# Taking Good Care

## Administration as Christian Formation

Jana Holiday

William B. Eerdmans Publishing Company
Grand Rapids, Michigan

Wm. B. Eerdmans Publishing Co.
2006 44th Street SE, Grand Rapids, MI 49508
www.eerdmans.com


Published 2026
Printed in the United States of America

32 31 30 29 28 27 26 1 2 3 4 5 6 7

ISBN 978-0-8028-8534-0

**Library of Congress Cataloging-in-Publication Data**

A catalog record for this book is available from the Library of Congress.

# Contents

Introduction: Growing Administrative Care 1

**Part 1: Work in an Ecosystem** 5

1. Good Decisions 9
2. Creating Good Change 23
3. Coordinating and Conflict 35

**Part 2: Cultivation** 49

4. The Stuff of Cultivation 55
5. Hospitable Administration 67
6. Proper Presence 79

**Part 3: Fruitfulness and Dominion** 91

7. "Taking Good Care" Versus Dominion 95
8. Figuring Out Fruit 107
9. How Do We Pray? 123

**Part 4: Imagination** 133

10. Imagination at Work 137

11. Design Thinking for Administrators 147

**Part 5: Administration in *Memento Mori*** 157

12. Nestedness 161

13. Succession Planning 173

14. Investing Beyond Our Years 183

Conclusion: Taken Care Of 193

*Acknowledgments* 197

*Notes* 199

# Introduction

## Growing Administrative Care

The Chicago Botanic Garden's paths wind around leisurely, hemmed in by evergreen plants warmly enfolding visitors and holding the nearby frantic highway buzz at bay. In contrast, Phoenix's Desert Botanical Garden is less embracing, more stark and wide open with a "What did you think you were going to get here?" posture. The endless sky eventually meets the desert horizon line, punctuated by cacti at various intervals. Coastal Maine Botanical Gardens brings a sense of the dramatic: pines tower above while the rolling hills only hint at what might be around the corner. Lush plants spill over the pathways. Each garden has its own life, its own culture, its own way of being in the world, cared for by experts, explored by visitors, doing what it is intended to do. Each garden thrives uniquely as its own ecosystem.

Organizations are much the same as these gardens—they are ecosystems that shape who we are and what we do. The presence of resources (or lack thereof) influences what grows, what our energy is best expended toward, and the level of strain on parts of the system. Each organization has a mission—something it is growing toward—that thing its stewards are expecting to see in the ecosystem. Ecosystems are complex yet integrated. They are interrelated networks in which we can dissect portions of the system, examine the granularity, or look at the environment from a high level, all of which are valuable. However, it is the personal that we will consider here, exploring what kind of people we need to be so that our particular organizational ecosystem thrives. What kind of people will take good care?

There are many entrance points to this question of organizational flourishing, but the door of administration is one that few excitedly walk through, so perhaps more attention should be paid to this particular function in an organizational ecosystem. Administration, at its most basic, is the stewardship of people, resources, and projects through a process. This happens everywhere, all the time. We are usually ambivalent toward administrative functions unless our expectations are not met—a process is more difficult than we thought it would be, it's easier to access resources than we assumed, or we end up on hold listening to endlessly monotonous music for an hour. In an organization there are people doing the stewarding of other people, resources, and projects, and it is their formation, as well as the formation they are providing, with which this book is concerned.

Ideally we come to all our work with our whole selves, but we are often tempted to put away our hearts or spirits when we open spreadsheets, in-boxes, or Google forms. Sometimes we even want to put away our brains just to get the task marked off as done. It need not be so. As we look at administration, particularly in the context of church and higher education, the goal is to pay attention to our fruitfulness, how effective and healthy we are, for the sake of the kingdom of God, for the witness of the church to Jesus in the world. Administration requires skills and capacities to faithfully steward the people, programs, and resources that are part of our responsibility and a theological and biblically informed perspective in pursuit of faithful work. And, the Spirit of God is present each moment. It is this core truth that drives the potential for formation and kingdom impact. If our goal is to be led by the Spirit of God, the niggling details matter.

The paradigm of the ecosystem works well when thinking about organizations and administration. A gardener doesn't just look after one plant but pays attention to what is going on around the plant. The gardener is checking the weather, evaluating hydration, noting the season coming and the weather trends. It is slow work to create a flourishing ecosystem, and we cannot predict with certainty how it will turn out. So much of it is outside of our control. It's the same for the administrator—it's not just one task, one email, but it's the whole integrated organization and person.

The gardener is part of the ecosystem, and what they bring into the space affects what grows and how it grows. If the gardener accidentally introduces an invasive species, it can be catastrophic. If the gardener forgets to turn on the sprinkler while on vacation, a withering death is forthcoming. The gardener can also bring in creative solutions, a vision for what growth could look like and a plan to get there. For those life-building opportunities, the gardener needs to grow also, as part of the ecosystem. It's about taking good care—of oneself, of others, and of the organization.

This book has five parts, each looking at an aspect of what an administrator does in the ecosystem. Scripture will anchor us with examples, principles, and perspective as we explore. Each chapter also includes an "ecosystem tool"—a practical directive for how to sharpen a skill, in addition to reflecting on the values and practices that form us as administrators. We'll begin with some of the foundational work in an organization's ecosystem—good decisions, creating good change, and addressing conflict. Then we will think about cultivation—paying attention to the air and soil in which an organization grows. In part 3, we will explore fruitfulness and dominion, diving deeper into what taking good care looks like (and what to avoid). Next, we will look at how to become open, creative, and imaginative administrators, developing our capacity to see what is possible. Finally, we will explore the idea of administration in *memento mori*. That is, in light of our death (or at least our eventual exit from an organization), how ought we to plan and prepare so that we bless those left behind?

While I am admittedly a terrible gardener, I love the work of administration. Solving problems *with* people and *for* people so that our organizations function as best as we can make them for the sake of the kingdom of God is my delight. I've done administration in a doctor's office, for a construction company, for a church, and mostly in Christian higher education. The students in my "Administration for

Ministry" classes tell me the course should be required for everyone because it is both practical and formative. My doctorate is in education with a focus on academic leadership (a.k.a. "administration") because I found that too often administration is understood as a necessary evil rather than a pursuit worthy of excellent theological and personal reflection and engagement.

"Taking good care" is rooted in the Edenic ideal for humanity, yet we do not live in Eden anymore. Often the notion of administration is met with groans, gritted teeth, and heavy sighs of resignation because it has to get done. My prayer is that this meditation—these exhortations on the formation God deems desirable in our ecosystems—would be met with hopefulness that while Eden is not possible for us, *life abundant* is. Life in Christ means a far better ecosystem than Eden. Life with the Holy Spirit means more fruitfulness than possible in Eden, because of the love of our Father, to whom all glory and praise is due.

# Part 1

## *Work in an Ecosystem*

Have you ever played detective as you walked into a church, a school, or the offices of an organization? Maybe you looked around at the signage and wondered who was in charge of an event advertised. Have you tried to see if you could walk into the office of the leader of the organization unhindered? To whom do people appeal when there is a difference of opinion on scheduling? In all these matters (and so many more) someone was (a) giving direction and (b) effecting change, with which (c) others may or may not have agreed. Administrators need competence in these three areas in the context of organizational ecosystems.

Working at a church as a young adult offered me an incredible experience of leadership in a complex environment. The church in which I served was multiethnic, and I had many experiences of being the minority because of my race and gender. That meant I often did not understand why programs were structured the way they were, how relationships were patterned, or why a particular approach would or would not work—all of which are stretching when you are the church administrator who is also overseeing small groups and spiritual formation! The Lord changed me so much during those years, and I am deeply grateful for those who invested in me—there were so many patient and gracious conversations.

In my early years at this church I served on a ministry team with a couple, Mary and Michael, who provoked feelings of irritability in me. This was certainly due to my immaturity and lack of cultural intelligence. They are Korean and I am not, and that cultural difference meant we diverged in how we thought about many things. That led to some friction as we worked together. We differed in how we gave direction and tried to change things. Their leadership did not match how I would do things, and I'm sure they had many concerns with how I led as well. I was fresh out of seminary and brimming with idealism!

We had an unexpected inroad to changing how we worked together. At our church we held a Thanksgiving banquet, and, as an expression of our multiethnic community, we served both traditional American food and Korean staples. Mary was in charge of the meal. That day an army of people converged on the church kitchen to help cook. Mary was an excellent leader, orchestrating all the disparate tasks needed to bring this meal together. When it was time to mix the *japchae* (a Korean noodle dish), Mary brought me over to the largest bowl I had ever seen, with a beach-ball-sized mountain of rice noodles, *bulgogi*, spinach, mushrooms, carrots, and sauce. Mary's direction was to "mix it up." I looked at this behemoth and realized the easiest way to do that was using my hands, so I just dove in and did my best. For years after that day Mary would describe that moment with admiration for me. I wonder if it was meaningful for her because it was a picture of what we wanted to do in that community—jump in and connect—and maybe she and others were worried that the non-Koreans would reject their culture and its expression in our church. I personified our communal experience of "getting our hands dirty."

By the grace of God, from that point, Mary and Michael and I began to change how we related to one other. We started intentionally spending time together, and I learned so much about Korean culture, their family culture, and them as individuals.

They welcomed me into their home at least once a week—often the three of us would walk together and sometimes share a meal. We talked about events at the church, how changes were being made, and where we wanted the future of the ministry to go. We developed a beautiful partnership. They gave me insight into Korean culture, and I helped them understand a few things about the younger generation as well as a multiethnic context.

Sadly, crises came to their lives and upended everything. I was one of the few people with whom they shared what happened. When Mary's mom died, I was part of the funeral service—the only non-Korean and person from our church involved. As it turned out, my formation as an administrator in this ecosystem was about me changing both for the sake of the church and the ministries we were building and for the sake of my friends. I could be the kind of person who more faithfully cared for them in that devastating season.

The gardener's role in an ecosystem is to provide direction toward growth and flourishing, which requires bringing new stimuli to the system, often leading to struggle over resources. Giving direction, effecting change, and navigating conflict in an organizational ecosystem is a very personal and costly endeavor, as I discovered through my relationship with Michael and Mary. It requires the formation of the gardener to faithfully do this work.

# 1

# Good Decisions

Meet the most underrated administrative consultant in the Bible: Jethro, Moses's father-in-law. The consultation occurs in Exodus 18:1–27, where Jethro shows himself to be someone who understands the importance of giving good direction in a challenging ecosystem.

Jethro knew Moses well. They spent forty years together after Moses ran away from Egypt and before he led the Israelites out of Egypt. Jethro took care of Moses's wife, Zipporah, and their two boys when Moses was preoccupied with Pharaoh and getting the Israelites out of Egypt. He delivered Moses's family back to him just when Moses needed wise counsel. As Jethro observed Moses in this new context, he could tell that Moses was heading down a difficult and draining administrative road as a leader.

> On the next day Moses sat to judge the people, and the people stood around Moses from morning until evening. When Moses' father-in-law saw all that he was doing for the people, he said, "What is this that you are doing for the people? Why are you sitting by yourself, and all the people stand around you from morning until evening?" Moses said to his father-in-law, "Because the people come to me to inquire of God. When they have a dispute, it comes to me and I decide between a man and his neighbor, and I make known the decrees of God and his laws." (Exodus 18:13–16)[1]

At that point Jethro stepped in with some wonderful common sense: this is a destructive setup! He did not attack Moses's character or his work, but rather he offered a creative suggestion for how decision making could be done better. It was a simple change in structure that involved organized delegation.

> "But you choose from the people capable men, God-fearing men, men of truth, those who hate bribes, and put them over the people as rulers of thousands, rulers of hundreds, rulers of fifties, and rulers of tens. They will judge the people under normal circumstances, and every difficult case they will bring to you, but every small case they themselves will judge, so that you may make it easier for yourself, and they will bear the burden with you. If you do this thing, and God so commands you, then you will be able to endure, and all these people will be able to go home satisfied." (Exodus 18:21–23)

Jethro cared for both Moses and the people by helping Moses build a healthy administrative culture of sharing the load of decision making. He helped develop in Moses a sense of hopefulness, counteracting the helplessness Moses felt. He helped foster abundance instead of scarcity, and he helped Moses move with agility rather than being bogged down.

Jethro influenced Moses's ministry habits so profoundly that his influence lasted for the next forty years. Deuteronomy 34:7 describes Moses's death: Moses was 120 years old, "yet his eyes were not weak nor his strength gone" (NIV). Jethro affected the ecosystem of the Israelites through his influence on how Moses gave direction. Moses, their great leader, finished strong (in part) because he listened to a wise counselor who could see a better way to make decisions and shape a healthier culture. Taking good care can bear fruit far beyond what we see. Let's learn how to build and refine these skills toward fruitfulness—who knows how God intends to use them?

### *Making Decisions*

Distilled down to its essence, the work of making decisions is the foundational piece of administration.[2] In organizational ecosystems, it makes sense that building a foundation with sound decision making leads to a system that does what we intend. For example, hiring and firing well (our tool-kit topic) prevents the ecosystem from being upended by a poor decision about who is or is not present in the ecosystem. Reflecting on and interrogating how we make decisions is the best way to improve our decision making.[3] Reflection that helps us understand our own agency leads to growth in our capacity to develop discernment.

How do you know what makes a good decision? Does it feel easy? Does it feel right? Does the supervisor or another stakeholder approve? How utilitarian are you in answering this question? The recognition of what makes a good decision could be context-dependent (someone in particular is pleased in a certain situation), or it could be a holistic sense that the decision is "proper." It could be about maintaining principles or life rules that guide decisions. It might not be about the pros outweighing the cons, but rather about conscience or the community agreeing.

The best way to begin is with the end in mind. What kind of a decision-maker do you want to be? Is that different from what kind of decision-maker your organization needs you to be? Two primary variables for decision making are pace and context. Do you make quick decisions that feel instinctual, or do you deliberate and ruminate? Do you ground yourself in a particular location and time, or do you hold to principles that transcend context? Are your decisions made collaboratively or independently? What happens when you experience decision fatigue? What matters to you in how you make decisions? How would you build a development plan for yourself that takes into account the kind of decision-maker you want to be? If it feels like your organization needs a different kind of decision-maker than you are naturally, how will you address that—do other people's expectations need to change, or will you learn a new way to make decisions?

Our work begins with a decision—do I preach on *x* or *y*? Should this event be on Monday or Tuesday? What email should I tackle first? While it is vital that we each make decisions reflecting our own leadership skills and personality, a scaffolding process for making decisions is possible. What follows is a modified scaffold described in Chip and Dan Heath's book *Decisive: How to Make Better Choices in Life and Work.*[4]

The impetus of decision making, of course, is that we encounter a choice. First, we set the parameters for the decision. The Heaths note two tendencies in our decision making: narrowing the frame of the choice at the cost of excluding real options, or setting the frame too large and inflating the scope (and therefore the importance) of the choice. For example, if I believe that the order in which I perform my mundane daily tasks is *the* signifier of a successful career, my perspective is misaligned out of this inflated scope. Whether I look at my calendar first or check my email is not the primary factor in building a career—it's not *that* important. Second, the Heaths tell us to analyze options but encourage us to account for confirmation bias (where we look for data that confirms what we already think to be the case). It is also helpful to assume the opposite of our potential bias so that not only do we aim for objectivity but we also develop empathy for other perspectives on an issue. Third, we make a choice! It's time for some action to take place. The Heaths warn against short-term emotions driving our choice, which could lead us in the wrong direction. However, it is also important to realize that those temporary emotions give us good information when they exist in an appropriate place. When our bodies and our brains give us information through adrenaline, stress, and even joy, we may as well interrogate the reasons for their presence rather than dismiss them as irrelevant, even if they only briefly hang around. Doing so may give us insight that strengthens our decision-making capacity. Finally, according to the Heaths, we are to live with the choice. Warning against overconfidence, they encourage us to be humble enough to change if needed. We must also account for the implications of underconfidence—if we hold back and don't live into the decision, that can set us and our team on an unhelpful trajectory. Incapacitating fear prohibits needed growth.

### *Community Formation in Discernment: Imagination*

Discernment is the process by which we determine a course of action. It's less technical than "decision making" and more about movement. Taking *good* care means that discernment is animated by faith and love. Foundationally, we must recognize that it is the Lord's perfect knowledge we seek and depend upon as fallen and finite humans. Discernment, thus, will never be without an element of trust, as we believe by faith that God speaks and that we have heard him rightly. But that does not mean that we are without confidence. Because we are *in* Christ (Romans 6:11), because we are indwelt by the Spirit of truth (John 14:17), a godly and wise process of discernment can be present. Secondly, discernment that seeks to be entirely "logical" without love is partially empty and corrupted. Identifying and reflecting on our love, as well as simply ensuring its presence, allows for holistic discerning to occur.

Even with faith and love present, practicing discernment still presents a significant challenge: we will always grapple with inadequacy and insecurity, given our human finitude. We cannot know completely, and sometimes that knowledge turns to fear and seeps into our bones, hindering us. Thus, discernment is always tethered to obedience. Usually we are okay with an element of obedience, at least in a small and controlled measure. These moments are more "hops" of faith than *leaps* of faith. However, it feels more likely than not that God uses "secret option C" in these experiences of discernment. We hope for plan A, figure out plan B, but at some point it becomes clear that the Lord had a hidden option all along that wasn't revealed until the perfect time (which of course was God's perfect time, not ours). In our finitude and fallenness, that obedience tether is indicative of a measure of humility. We are image-bearers, and our confidence comes through that identifier so that we receive the joy of belonging and value to which nothing else compares.

Theologian Lester Ruiz observes that "one needs to 'tell one's story in the light of someone else's story' in all their complex, asymmetrical, contingent, contestational, even incommensurable character."[5] In communities we practice the skill of both listening to others' stories and learning to speak our own stories with an ear toward what formation occurs within it. This community formational discernment is an invitation to see beyond facts to the meaning within the collective story. It's like listening to the unique facets of the ecosystem to understand the meaning of the whole—but that is indeed a difficult task. However, imagination is just the tool that we need.

When people feel busy, overwhelmed, and oversaturated, we have the opportunity to help them imaginatively pursue participation in God's work and avoid the things that dissuade us from living with discernment. Our culture ensnares us by suggesting that we ought to desire everything in immeasurable amounts. Perhaps the great gift of imagination in an organizational ecosystem is that it can serve to help us find our true desires. Imagination is the capacity that fosters the ability to see beyond what is present to a different future. It creates space for freedom and hopefulness even while accounting for the fallen world in which we live.

Imagination helps us see rightly and become the right kind of person. Part of the work is painting a hope-filled vision of identity, community, and work—imagining a kingdom-shaped life. We want to guide others toward living with one foot in the present reality and one foot in the eschatological reality, moving ever toward that side of things, keeping the long view in sight. We cannot do this without imaginative seeing.

Discernment ought to be about enhancing our participation in God's work, helping us become better kingdom citizens. Building a rhythm of the practice of listening prayer, acknowledging ourselves (our biases and background, etc.), and humility in recognizing sin and our need for repentance contribute to our discernment. Dallas Willard exhorts us: "We must thoughtfully take that Word in, dwell upon it, ponder its meaning, explore its implications."[6] It is only then that we can make "a critical reflection in faith and humility that enables us to more fully be disciples of Jesus Christ and fulfill the call to be men and women of love."[7] Discernment by kingdom-shaped imaginative people contributes to wise and excellent care for the organizational ecosystem.

What a wonderful ideal. However, the world in which we live seems to strive against this. Even with the best of intentions, why does poor discernment still take place? Perhaps we experience fatigue related to a lack of boundaries, or overstimulation. Maybe our lack of good discernment is due to a pattern of inaction, maybe a lack of imagination. Are we enslaved to fear, or have we changed to meet someone else's expectations? Maybe we grapple with perfectionism and are crippled by the potential of making a mistake. Poor discernment is also learned through family, church, or other role models. Anger, unresolved traumas, or even inappropriate views of God or his will can lead to poor choices.

One temptation often present in American Christian culture is to see a difficult situation as something that could not be from God due to how painful or strenuous it is. Scripture calls us to a different perspective. Consider Genesis 13 when Abraham and Lot part ways over a land dispute. Abraham offered Lot the choice of which area he wanted. Lot chose the direction that seemed easiest, containing the most resources. What if instead he had chosen the more difficult path, potentially offering the "better" option to Abraham, the father figure who had done so much for him? Lot would have been forced to grow much deeper in his faith, trusting in the One who could provide for him and lead him, and Lot would see Yahweh's *hesed*—his covenant faithfulness—day after day. Lot's hope was for this life alone, and the eschatologically hopeful life that the difficult choice would have cultivated in him was a missed opportunity.

In reflecting on discernment, Marva Dawn observes, "What has kept me from discerning the abundance of God's goodness has often been that I simply don't love God enough."[8] It was in this particular season of her life, as she chose to engage in worship more deeply, that a sense of humility and deep trust in the sovereignty of God was fostered.[9] Communities share language and stories about how worship "puts us in our place." I remember attending a gospel choir concert one December when I worked at a college. I watched the faces of the choir members during a song about praising God when crossing mountains. Not only did tears stream down students' faces as they sang, but the audience resonated with the message, as our students and staff neared the end of an exceptionally difficult semester. We needed to be given the words of both what God had done for us and what our response ought to be. When that happened, it was a powerful and Spirit-filled moment.

### *Delegation*

Taking our cues from Jethro and Moses, wise administrators who are taking good care of their ecosystems must account for delegation—through our skills in both performing and receiving delegation. We must guard against the pendulum of overdelegation or underdelegation in an organization's system. How do we hit the happy medium between potential laziness and responsibility shirking from overdelegation and the overwork and burnout potential of underdelegation? Here is a general process for delegating with good care:

1. Name the goals of the office/department/organization—make sure each unit's goals connect with the overall mission.
2. Choose what can be delegated wisely. What can only be done by you, what can you train someone to do, and what can you immediately hand off?
3. Take into account the skills and abilities of the workers in that unit to reach those goals. Are the right people around, and are they tasked with the right things? Ideally tasks are given according to strength—if someone does not possess the skill set needed and it's not the right thing to teach them, they should not receive the delegated task.[10]
4. Once you have the person and task set, trust them. Give encouragement and credit liberally. Also, give authority and responsibility—the stakes should be real, not just busywork.

5. Hold yourself to account for having the right structure, support, and challenge. Everyone needs all three—enough structure to provide direction and boundaries, the right support to keep them going, and sufficient challenge to provide adequate motivation and engagement. It's helpful to think of these as making up a stool. Some days more of one leg may be needed than the other, but all should be present.[11]
6. Always give feedback (positive and constructive) for the sake of the project and for the sake of developing the person.

The hope is that our delegation reflects the fruit that was born through Jethro in Moses's ministry. When the load is shared, hopefulness is more likely to be present because of healthy team engagement (rather than helplessness). Because of the potential for positive investment, catalytic work, and momentum, a feeling of abundance might develop rather than a feeling of scarcity. With the right structure and the appropriate margin, more agility is usually demonstrated and the organizational ecosystem flourishes.

### *Tool Kit: Hiring and Firing*

As an illustration of some of these decision-making and discernment principles, let's look at hiring and firing. We want these experiences to result in the right decision, so excellent decision making is needed all along the way. As several key aspects are highlighted below, there is much room for taking good care in the process.

One of the more difficult things in the hiring process is discerning if a candidate has the necessary intangible characteristics. I think about three categories when getting to know a candidate: (1) Do they have the confidence to do the job and the capacity to grow the position? (2) Are they teachable? Humility is such a vital part of being on a healthy team, and when that is coupled with an eagerness to learn, I get excited! (3) Do I want to spend time investing in them? Even if they meet those first two qualifications, if I'm put off by some things about their personality and cannot see myself getting over them, it's not a wise hire. Of course, I need to reflect on the legitimacy of my discomfort—what do I need to internally resolve, and what is a deal-breaker?

Let's go through some general guidelines for hiring:

1. Length of wait to gather candidates
    a. Options: publish how long the window will be open (applications accepted for six weeks); keep it open until you have a good number of candidates (five to ten); or keep it open until you have the position hired. The right option will often depend on how competitive the job is and what time line is available.
    b. The most valuable thing to know about the overall process of hiring: it always takes longer than we expect.
2. Goals of an interview
    a. Get to know the candidate.
    b. Help the candidate become acquainted with the organization and department, and if appropriate, with the supervisor or team with whom they will work, or both.
    c. Most importantly, shape the expectations of the relationship and the job. An interview's main purpose is to protect everyone from a charge of baiting and switching down the road.
3. Kinds of questions to ask in an interview
    a. Case studies are the best format of gathering information because they help you see the candidate in practice.
    b. Ask the candidate to tell you a story about their involvement in a leadership role in the past and then have them reflect on it. For example, "Tell us about when you were leading in a stressful situation—what would you do differently next time?" That gives their benchmark for what stress is, what their leadership and coping skills are, and how practiced they are at reflection.
    c. Ask tried-and-true interview questions if you wish, but always drill down and ask off-the-wall questions. I was asked what I was most afraid of when I was interviewing for my

first job in higher education. I thought deeply and answered honestly (I was concerned I would bring dysfunction to a healthy team).

d. Always interview with someone else so you have a conversation partner afterward—you may miss something important, or your own biases may get in the way of an accurate assessment.

e. Keep in mind that you see only a small fraction of who the person is in an interview. The goal is to mine for the most truthful expression of who that person is and how they will do the job.

4. References

   a. Always call the reference to cover yourself, and document the conversation.

   b. Especially for high-impact positions, ask the reference for someone else they suggest you talk to. (I got called for an old boss's boss when he changed jobs—we hadn't worked together in eleven years, and they had some specific questions for me about how he handled a unique issue.)

   c. Ask for stories from the reference about the candidate. Ask if they would hire that person. Ask if they have any reservations about the candidate working with specific populations (especially vulnerable ones).

   d. Remember that the stakes are low for the reference, so they may not be completely truthful with you. They may potentially have less than honorable motivations for their answers. They may want the candidate out of their organization. They may be the best friend of the candidate and don't disclose that. Assume they are biased, but that doesn't mean you can't ferret out helpful information. Also, assume that whatever you ask about will get back to the candidate.

5. Social media

   a. Advertise the position on social media if you are so inclined.

   b. Do whatever research you can about the candidate on social media, potentially even hiring a firm to do this for you. In this day and age, that's worth it. Posts and comments matter!

6. Contracts
   a. Always put the offer in writing—a candidate might be excited to get the offer and not remember correctly the details of the position.
   b. Always get the candidate to reply in agreement in writing. This may preclude a he said/she said situation.
7. Things to not ask in an interview
   a. Always review current federal and state guidance prior to an interview. If a candidate brings a topic up and shares information with you, you can engage with them on it, but be very cautious.
   b. Avoid asking about: age, race, ethnicity, color, gender, sex, sexual orientation or gender identity, country of origin, birthplace, religion (unless that is a stated job requirement), disability, marital status, family status, pregnancy, salary history (in some states), arrest record (sometimes).

A couple of administrative nonnegotiables apply to all employees, but they are particularly important when working with an employee whose involvement with the organization becomes tenuous. The most important thing is to write everything down—from job description and expectations to reviews and plans for employee improvement. Second, it is possible to help someone come to the conclusion themselves that they are not the right fit for the job or organization. Often people will want to resign to save face. Sometimes you can incentivize that with better severance if they resign. Separation agreements are contracts that lay out what the organization will do for the person leaving and what the person is asked to do—they include information about the severance, warning against defamation, and agreements about nondisclosure.[12]

Here are some general guidelines when firing someone:

1. Do your utmost to maintain the person's dignity and value when having these conversations. They are created in the image of God,

and, even if we are frustrated at their performance and they've caused us and our organizations a lot of problems, we still need to treat them as precious and full of worth.

2. Advocate for severance packages and benefits to continue as long as possible. The goal is to help bridge between jobs.
3. Do not leave room for negotiation. The decision must already have been made when the meeting is scheduled. Think through ahead of time what objections or concerns the person will bring up. Have separation agreements ready if applicable.
4. Explain the communication plan at that time: what stakeholders will be told when, how, and by whom.
5. Be sure to explain what you will ask the person to do after that conversation (immediately leave, two weeks to wrap up, six months from now, etc.). If they are to immediately leave, access to information and resources (files, email, keys, etc.) needs to be removed at that time.
6. Make sure the meeting is brief, but also give them adequate time to ask questions once we give the news. If they are not being fired immediately, it's better to have these meetings earlier in the week rather than on Friday (people stew over the weekend, and it's more likely someone will come in Monday angry).
7. There is a good chance we will not be liked by a number of people when we fire someone (or encourage them to leave). Even if the employee seems fine with it, assume their spouse won't be. Remember, most people won't know the full story, and we cannot tell them because so much is confidential due to employment law.

What does God think about firing people? Administrators are stewards of their people, resources, and organizations. There's a balance in that. Are we being faithful stewards when we keep someone on the payroll of a church who isn't doing the work of the ministry? Are we giving people the support they need to do their jobs well before we evaluate them (it ought to be fair)? Is someone abusing others in their position? Being a good steward means firing a harmful person. Much wisdom is needed in balancing these areas. Sometimes the loving thing is to let someone go. We might see that they are not in a place where they are thriving, and they (or you) are unwilling or unable to participate in a growth plan to get them where they need to be. Preserving someone's dignity means that we see them honestly. Finally, we need to be aware of our own emotional state. Unreflected-upon sin or anger is not helpful. Anger is a tool when it is righteous. It is a weapon when it is unrighteous and will harm us and others. Letting someone go ought to be an act of love.

### *Questions for Reflection*

1. Have you benefited from a Jethro in your life? How did that relationship shape your administrative leadership? Has God invited you into a Jethro role for someone else? How can you steward that opportunity faithfully?
2. What matters to you in how you make decisions? Do you want to be instinctual or slowly reflective, or a mix? Is your approach appropriately collaborative?
3. How do you communicate your decisions? If anything bothers you in your approach, how could you develop different capacities for decision making? Discernment is integrally connected to obedience. Take a few minutes to reflect on the posture of your heart—is there anything you've said no to that God may be inviting you to say yes to?
4. On a spectrum of overdelegation to underdelegation, where do you most naturally fall? What are the implications of that for your context? Is there an adjustment you could make that would be a helpful change for your ecosystem?
5. Have your own experiences of being hired or fired (whether positive or negative) inappropriately affected your approach to hiring and firing others? Be sure to process through these experiences to more healthily engage in these practices.

2

# Creating Good Change

Perhaps the most pertinent characteristic of an ecosystem is the interrelated nature of what goes on within it. One small change affects something else, which affects something else, and so on. It is the "butterfly flaps its wings and is felt on the other side of the world" phenomenon. We might contextualize that to an "I change one thing on a form and the whole event crumbles" circumstance. Understanding ourselves as we change, as well as what change feels like in our organizations, contributes to our capacity to nurture flourishing in and around us. Change in an organizational ecosystem can feel overwhelming, so the more we can identify the aspects of the change that may help us navigate it, the more we can employ it for the health of the organization.

### *Leading Ourselves Through Change*

What happens *to us* when we experience change? We are often tempted to remain tethered to our "same old" leadership tendencies and gifts with which we are most comfortable, thereby missing out on growth opportunities when change pops up. Sometimes fear or even laziness shapes our response to change. Usually we have a choice to become bitter, to stick our heels in the ground to avoid the change, or to welcome it.

The apostle Paul began his life with one extreme posture and ended it with a completely different one. Consider his beginning approach in Galatians 1:13–14: "For you have heard of my former way of life in Judaism, how I was savagely persecuting the church of God and trying to destroy it. I was advancing in Judaism beyond many of my contemporaries in my nation, and was extremely zealous for the traditions of my ancestors." Paul's goal was to destroy the Christian church. His career and firmly held religious beliefs drove him. His loyalty to his ancestors and teachers ran deep. In Acts 8:1 we find that Paul approvingly watched the church's first martyr, Stephen, face death.

Paul's "after" in this story is equally dramatic. Second Corinthians 12:9 tells us that Paul had reached a humble acceptance of God's will for his life, embracing that God's grace was sufficient for him. In that same chapter we are led to understand that Paul was willing to expend himself for an ungrateful and difficult church, grieving over their sin. What a change! "Everything we do, dear friends, is for your strengthening" (2 Corinthians 12:19).

*What happened in the middle to make him so different?*

Galatians 1 gives us helpful insight into this: "The one who set me apart from birth and called me by his grace was pleased to reveal his Son in me so that I could preach him among the Gentiles" (Galatians 1:15–16).

Three aspects of Paul's experience led to his formation through change. First, *Paul recognized that God set him apart,* as evidenced by his dramatic conversion experience on the road to Damascus. God intervened in his life and gave him a new job—he was to go and preach to the gentiles (Acts 9:15–16). The essence of set-apart-ness has to do with our mission, recognizing that God has a purpose for us. Paul testified in Acts 20:24, "I do not consider my life worth anything to myself, so that I may finish my task and the ministry that I received from the Lord Jesus, to testify to the good news of God's grace." He had a sense that his life was not his own.

Second, *Paul recognized that he was called by God's grace.* This new life (even with all the difficulties inherent in it) was far better than what Paul had going before. God's goodness rescued him, and his grace extended eternal life to Paul: "For I am the least of the apostles, unworthy to be called an apostle, because I persecuted the church of God. But by the grace of God I am what I am, and his grace to me has not been in vain. In fact, I worked harder than all of them—yet not I, but the grace of God with me" (1 Corinthians 15:9–10). It's the kindness of God that changes us.

Finally, *Paul met Jesus*. Knowing Jesus as friend, brother, Savior, and so much more cannot help but transform us. Paul never recovered from the amazement that Jesus had been revealed to him on the road to Damascus. Paul had experienced what it means to know Christ and to join his life. He practiced what he preached: "Use your freedom as an opportunity to . . . through love serve one another" (Galatians 5:13).

Galatians 2 describes a conflict between Peter and Paul that resulted in a major change in each of their ministries. Peter was acting hypocritically, and Paul sought to correct that behavior because this was a central issue in their work as ministers of the gospel. If the community of Jews and gentiles were at odds over the gospel, clearly Christianity had less power than was purported. Paul explained what the problem was with Peter's actions and how that impacted their vision and mission as a movement.

It's worth noting what Paul did not do in this situation. He did not become upset that Peter (who had known Jesus longer!) didn't get it. He did not become arrogant that God gave him his own special mission to the gentiles, nor did he avoid the conflict and assume that someone else would address it.

Paul responded in a manner that was caring for both Peter and the community—he publicly addressed the hypocrisy. Peter's sanctification, as well as the growth of the community on this issue, was too important to be dealt with behind closed doors.[1] Paul helped them see that the heart of the issue was how they were living out the gospel. It's not about an action, but rather a value and a posture. Paul showed how their conduct could glorify God and make much of Christ.

Consider 2 Corinthians 5:14–20:

> For the love of Christ controls us, since we have concluded this, that Christ died for all; therefore all have died. And he died for all so that those who live should no longer live for themselves but for him who died for them and was raised. So then from now on we acknowledge no one from an outward human point of view. Even though we have known Christ from such a human point of view, now we do not know him in that way any longer. So then, if anyone is in Christ, he is a new creation; what is old has passed away—look, what is new has come! And all these things are from God who reconciled us to himself through Christ, and who has given us the ministry of reconciliation. In other words, in Christ God was reconciling the world to himself, not counting people's trespasses against them, and he has given us the message of reconciliation. Therefore we are ambassadors for Christ, as though God were making his plea through us. We plead with you on Christ's behalf, "Be reconciled to God!"

What can happen to us when we faithfully walk through change and the conflict that often comes with it? We become ministers of reconciliation and Christ's ambassadors, embodying the gospel in our very being. What a high calling and privilege in administration and everyday life.

### *Change Models*

Personal change often intersects with organizational change. For example, when someone who cares for the ecosystem learns a new skill or grows in their capacity for work, that can lead to adapting the system. Sometimes outside factors lead to change in the ecosystem, which requires change in the people who make up the ecosystem. Coping with change means recognizing it as such, interpreting what is going on around us accurately, which mediates stress on the system.

Let's start with the building blocks needed to create change. Change requires:

- an agent (someone empowered to actually do or lead the thing),
- determination (will or some sort of energy source),
- sustainability (continuing resources),
- team (in an organization, we can't be the only one rooting for it).

Let's say those four ingredients are reasonably attainable. Their initiation is dependent on some motivating catalyst—maybe a desire to do things better, or external factors like laws, crises, or culture shifts. We tend to function under a general model of change. The right model depends on the character of our organizational ecosystems.

Our first model is one by Kurt Lewin, a German American psychologist who worked in the 1940s.[2] Lewin's model is fairly straightforward and is generally how most people think about change. There are clear differences between steps in the model and set responsibilities for the leader. Lewin described three stages an organization needs to work through to bring about change:

1. *Unfreeze.* The first step is to overcome inertia and mental blocks to change. His remedies include telling employees (or stakeholders) about a change as soon as possible. Making sure others understand the change and how it is likely to affect them contributes to a smooth process. The leader ought to be positive about the change and, if stakeholders find it difficult, able to describe how the organization will help them cope. Leaders create space for concerns to be raised and questions asked. The process is meant to be transparent and attentive to concerns.
2. *Change.* The old ways of doing things will soon be gone, and that can lead to confusion and chaos. The key to implementing change is building on successes. As stakeholders see the change achieving desirable results, they are more likely to go along with it and even embrace it. To induce changes in behavior, the change effort should include tangible or intangible rewards for the desired behavior.
3. *Freeze.* This new mind-set that the organization has engaged in

> must be cemented. The change process is complete only when stakeholders make the new behavior part of their routine. Lewin notes that backsliding is a natural response; therefore, supervisors need to keep everyone on track. An important part of refreezing is for employees to be rewarded for behavior that shows they have made the desired change.[3]

Traditional organizations tend to work best with Lewin's model of change. Also, for leaders who are newer to leading change, this is often the best model. It's based on common sense and how we generally function in our personal lives through change. Having specified stages allows for clarity and greater capacity for unified movement together.

A more complex and dynamic model was created by John Kotter, a businessman and academic, who described a change model that closely attends to the management of energy and focus in an organization as the leader responsively directs change.[4]

He suggests eight steps for leading change:

1. Establish a sense of urgency. This is the motivation for movement—a bold, aspirational opportunity. The goal is to explain why acting immediately is required.
2. Form a powerful guiding coalition. This is a group of people who will join the cause because they see the urgency of the issue. These people will help to coordinate the movement.
3. Form a strategic vision and initiatives. This is the thing to work toward that people can grasp onto. This step tells people how this will be different from the past.
4. Enlist a volunteer army. Now we are working on a larger scale—change needs lots of people to join for it to genuinely take root.
5. Enable action by removing barriers. Remove inefficiencies and unhelpful hierarchies, as these are the main issues.
6. Generate short-term wins. Kotter notes that "wins are the molecules of results," and this creates energy and focus.

7. Sustain acceleration. His suggestion is to be relentless and not take your foot off the gas pedal—produce more and more change until the vision is reality.
8. Institutionalize new approaches. This is about making them last. He directs us to "articulate the connections between new behaviors and organizational success, making sure they continue until they become strong enough to replace old habits."

Ecosystems in which the leader is inclined to and has the capacity to move in and among the stakeholders work well with Kotter's model. So much of the success of this way of leading change depends on the leader understanding the pulse of the organizational ecosystem. This takes a high level of engagement and relationality. Leading a dispersed organization rather than one that is centrally located could make Kotter's model more difficult to achieve.

An example of a change model that considers organizational culture and unique attentiveness of the leader of an organization is Heifetz and Linsky's. Ronald Heifetz and Marty Linsky wrote a survival guide for leaders, in which, according to their model, leaders must make sure they understand the *nature* of the change they are going for.[5] There are two main kinds of change: adaptive and technical. Adaptive change "requires individuals throughout the organization to alter their ways; as the people themselves are the problem, the solution lies with them." Technical change means that "technical problems, while often challenging, can be solved applying existing know-how and the organization's current problem-solving processes."

Heifetz and Linsky describe techniques to overcome disequilibrium caused by change. When change causes unsettledness and instability, here's what can be done:

- Operate in and above the fray. They describe perspectives that are both on the dance floor and in the balcony—leaders need to be present in both spaces, as participants and observers, respectively.
- Court the uncommitted. Their suggestion is to keep the opposition

close as well as those who are on the fence. The value of people must be present. Adopt the behavior you want from others and acknowledge your responsibility in whatever the issue is.

- Cook the conflict. Most organizations see conflict as dangerous, but if we manage it wisely, it can be used to bring change. The challenge is to keep the heat high enough to motivate but low enough to prevent explosions. The way to do that is to embody hope, not fear. Humor and managing pace are helpful for lowering the temperature. Sometimes complaints are fine because that is what is needed to get stuff done.
- Place the work where it belongs. The change leader needs to transfer problem solving to others often, so that they are appropriately empowered and not dependent.
- Manage yourself. Restrain your desire for control and need for importance—usually control and self-importance are related. Remember that dependence on the leader can be detrimental because the team needs to be able to function adequately even if the leader is not around.
- Finally, anchor yourself. This includes having a safe place of reflection, renewal, and recalibration. A confidant is needed, along with separation of personal self from professional self.

Heifetz and Linsky's model requires the most from a leader—to look through multiple lenses and to envision multiple steps ahead of where most people currently are. The model needs a leader able to take risks and an ecosystem capable of absorbing additional stress that comes with risk taking and turning up the heat. It also requires significant emotional and social intelligence to manage oneself with all that is going on. An organization with stakeholders who have a high level of emotional intelligence will do well with Heifetz and Linsky's model.

There are seasons in which we are not leading change ourselves but rather experiencing it—in those seasons, it's helpful to be familiar with the potential ways in which we ourselves may be led. Familiarity with these models (as exemplars of the primary ways we think about change in organizations) can help us at least recognize which models our leaders tend toward, and possibly anticipate their next moves. It's more difficult to progress through the change when we are in a state of shock since the change depends on us enacting our normal roles in the system. The more we can name the change going on around us, the more likely we can contribute positively to the organizational ecosystem.

### *Mind-sets of Change*

The majority of change management is dealing with our own head-space so we can deal with the emotions of others. There are two main approaches to walking through change. The first option is to plan out things as much as possible, with due dates, project plans, and lots of getting things ready. Usually not much space for iteration is included because the goal is to get it right the first time. Everyone knows what the task is, and maybe it takes longer to get there, but the team knows the goal. There are stages and gates and postmortems, and most of the growth happens by thinking through the problem. If you've seen a Gantt chart, that's indicative of this first approach—clear phases, set roles, and stages toward the end.

The second option is focused on iteration and development such that the goal is to try a lot of options—learning happens by doing something. There's plenty of failure involved, and reflection on what's happened. There are a lot of potential solutions to the problem, which itself is usually not modified. It's more fluid, requiring flexibility and a different kind of communication that includes emotional support in the presence of setbacks and inadequacy.

What is required of us as leaders or team members with each option? Both hold deep opportunities to trust God and listen to the Spirit—whether it's in the planning stage of the first option or the "try anything" season of the second. Recognizing which style works best within our ecosystem is helpful discernment—and also recognizing how to stretch the system to what is less natural for it is important. The goal is not to get really good at one way of doing change, but rather the goal is faithfulness and readiness for whatever God has in terms of kingdom work.

### *Tool Kit: Policy Writing*

Policies are a little like grocery lists—we need them so we don't forget what's important, so we live within our means, and so we don't get lost in the options. Included in the process of instantiating change is codifying various aspects of the organization so that everyone understands what to do in situations and how to respond to common concerns. That's why we write policies—so consistency is maintained and, when changes are made, everyone understands the anchors in the new iteration.

Policies really can be both freeing and constricting, and the key to landing in the right place is to recognize that policies are meant to benefit all of us—the organization itself and those it serves. Here's the thing that is too easy to forget: policies can be changed if they do not do what we want them to do. A healthy organization has a clear process for how to do that and people willing to walk through that process.

Clarity is absolutely what makes a good policy. Policies name the goal and provide clear steps toward that goal so that misunderstandings are all but impossible! Good policies are fair—can you imagine working in an organization where one manager gave five weeks of paid time off, versus another who gave just one? All parties are protected from abuse and from being taken advantage of. While this may be a minority opinion, an organization with clear policies should also have space for grace—that unearned favor that's pure blessing for someone else. That's life-giving for those enacting the policy. When we received COVID funds from the government, once we met all the requirements of the disbursements, there were some funds left. I will never forget the joy the financial aid director and I had when we got to tell a very lovely student with very few resources that we were using that extra money to pay off her debt. Kleenex were passed around for all.

How does one write a good policy? Always start with the end in mind—what are the goals of the policy? We have to know for whom the policy is being written—internal or external, clients, stakeholders, etc.—the audience matters. It's always wise to research similar examples of what is needed so that you can contextualize for your organization, or to ask AI to write your first draft. Of course, always ask permission if you are going to significantly borrow from another policy and give credit if needed. After you create your own draft, edit it while wearing the metaphorical glasses of those who will use the policy. Have people in the organization but not directly affected by the policy content review it. Depending on the stakes, it might be helpful to have legal counsel review it. Then, bring the policy to relevant bodies for approval as needed and make edits, even opening it up for public comment if appropriate. It might be wise to have legal counsel review it again before the final approval. Publication and communication of the policy is also part of developing it, as are reviews and updates. Regular reviews ensure that the policies are doing what we intend for them to do and so that we do not have a slew of outdated documents.

Policies can be changed, and policies can be a blessing!

### *Questions for Reflection*

1. Overall, are you resilient in seasons of change? What in particular challenges your flourishing in these seasons?
2. Paul's experience was recognizing he was called by God, set apart, and had encountered Jesus—that transformed his life. As you reflect on God's intervention in your life, pause to worship and to ensure that you are remembering this great work.
3. Given your ecosystem, which change model do you gravitate toward (Lewin's simple model, Kotter's dynamic model, or Heifetz

and Linsky's attentive leader model)? Do you feel equipped to lead and serve within those models?

4. Which of the two mind-sets of change (thorough planning versus try anything) feels most natural to you? Is this a season where you could focus on growing so that you also have proficiency in the other one? What would developing yourself look like if you did so?
5. What's your role in developing policies for your organization? What could be sharpened in terms of your abilities and involvement?

3

# Coordinating and Conflict

In the midst of change there often emerges some sort of conflict—the kind where people grasp for power, emotions are charged, and the implications of no resolution are heart wrenching. The work of administration means recognizing potential conflict and preparing to minimize the parts that may not be necessary, all the while readying to wisely address it, should the moment come. It's coordinating people, plans, schedules, and conversations. We don't always think about conflict as needing those coordinating skills, but a healthy ecosystem ought to have an internal mechanism so that different organisms communicate with one another when something isn't going well. That way the other organisms can help fix the issue or assist in whatever adaptation may be necessary.

My five-year-old nephew got a terrarium for his birthday, complete with dinosaur figurines and chia seeds that are supposed to grow. As we put it together, it struck me that each item included in the kit was meant to contribute to the growth of those seeds. We put a layer of rocks underneath the peat soil to account for an overenthusiastic kid who overwaters. There's a lid on top of the terrarium to account for the forgetful kid who underwaters, helping to capture whatever moisture is there. Each item is necessary for success. The terrarium works as a whole to account for situations when resources are abundant as well as when they are scarce—the basic cause of terrarium (and organizational ecosystem) destruction. Organizational conflict often arises from resource scarcity in some form (insufficient time, money, or leadership), and if we can coordinate well given the lack, growth may still occur.

Acts 6 provides a beautiful example of wise response to conflict for the sake of the gospel. The people we read about in the first part of Acts experienced a total reorientation in every aspect of their lives. Because of Jesus, everything changed: relationships (loving neighbors), finances (giving with no thought of return and to whoever had need), how we relate to God (as loving Father), and how we work in the world (as unto the Lord). This newly convened church had to figure out leadership, who then had to help the community discern what to do with whatever resources they had—often a source of conflict.

Consider Acts 6:1–7:

> Now in those days, when the disciples were growing in number, a complaint arose on the part of the Greek-speaking Jews against the native Hebraic Jews, because their widows were being overlooked in the daily distribution of food. So the twelve called the whole group of the disciples together and said, "It is not right for us to neglect the word of God to wait on tables. But carefully select from among you, brothers, seven men who are well-attested, full of the Spirit and of wisdom, whom we may put in charge of this necessary task. But we will devote ourselves to prayer and to the ministry of the word." The proposal pleased the entire group, so they chose Stephen, a man full of faith and of the Holy Spirit, with Philip, Prochorus, Nicanor, Timon, Parmenas, and Nicolas, a Gentile convert to Judaism from Antioch. They stood these men before the apostles, who prayed and placed their hands on them. The word of God continued to spread, the number of disciples in Jerusalem increased greatly, and a large group of priests became obedient to the faith.

There was a problem with resource division related to ethnic background. The Greeks thought the Hebrews were discriminating against them when food was being distributed to widows. The solution to this charge was a committee—normal practice in organizations. However, it's the ethnic makeup of this committee that is so profound: Stephen, Philip, Prochorus, Nicanor, Timon, Parmenas, Nicolas from Antioch (a convert to Judaism)—all seven of them were Greek. Here is why this is so meaningful:

1. The disciples trusted those in their organization. They could have easily done a 4-3 split between Jews and Greeks, or made it a group of eight so there could be four of each. Instead, they gave *complete* control over to those who raised the concern, trusting them to lead as part of the resolution to the conflict. Think about how radical that is—to trust those who complain to fix the issue by handing over all the power. This passage gives no indication that it was a bitter walking away in frustration—rather, there was a genuine gift of power. The disciples graciously gave away all the power and the responsibility, and no one lost in this scenario.
2. Often the interpretation of this passage is assumed to be about division of labor and dignity for all roles in the organization, giving freedom to those who have specific gifts or callings so they can engage in those. That is accurate; however, let's not miss the denouement of the passage in Acts 6:7: "The word of God continued to spread; the number of the disciples increased greatly in Jerusalem, and a great many of the priests became obedient to the faith." Because the disciples stewarded their power well (which in this case meant releasing control of the money), the church grew.
3. It's curious that the writer of Acts specifically mentions priests here. I wonder if the political maneuvering described was so powerful, so clearly and appealingly countercultural, that one of the most difficult-to-reach demographics in this society surprisingly began following Jesus because of this situation. The priests were the leaders of the opposition. They were the ones who had the power in their religious organization (and in the culture at large). They knew better than anyone what it meant for the disciples to

> reorganize in such a fashion. How could they not see the incredible ministry of the word of God in this simple resolution? This wasn't just the disciples handing off minor tasks so they could have more time for the ministry of the word—this was evidence of the gospel in the life of the community and organization. It is why faithfully stewarding power in conflict is so important.

So often the word "conflict" suggests people sitting across a table explaining their side of things and then walking away with a semblance of resolution. Or walking away with deeper wounds because of what was said (or not said). Thinking about our organizations as ecosystems means that we seek a deeper level of understanding. We reflect on how the conflict emerged in that particular ecosystem, as well as personal considerations such as how we might be holding on to power or responsibility unnecessarily, how assumptions of scarcity are impacting things, and what the radical nature of the gospel of Jesus might be inviting us toward. We will unpack these as we go, but first, let's explore the concepts of politics and power.

### *Framing Politics*

Based on a number of qualifiers such as age, gender, ethnicity, or family background, the word "power" may leave you with a negative connotation. You may or may not recognize yourself as holding power in your ecosystem—everyone holds some sort of power in their position in the organization to some degree (whether volunteer or paid), even if it's simply the power to walk away. When we don't recognize the power inherent in administrative tasks, we run a far greater risk of abusing it or squandering it. It is far better to recognize that with the assumption of stewardship comes power.[1]

Often the term "politics" has a negative connotation as well—sometimes with surprising strength in election years. What happens if negativity overwhelms us and we eschew proper understanding of both power and politics? One might question why in a book on administration we have to talk about power and politics. They are propitious realities in our organizations, and learning to recognize the structures in which we are a part is vital to our capacity to navigate our ecosystems. Put more staunchly, *how we navigate power and politics has a direct correlation to how effective we are and the tenor of the effectiveness that results from our engagement.*

Navigating issues of conflict (and therefore power and politics) is always about stewardship—taking care of the people and situations before us. It is also always about love—which is self-giving and self-sacrificial. Holding on to these anchors in no way allows for permitting others to abuse power, but rather obligates us to respond. If I love my neighbor, I cannot stand by and watch them misuse resources or relationships. Rather I must understand my organization and the system in which I am a part to navigate how to best address the conflict or abuse.

We are corrupted people, and our expressions of power will be corrupted because of sin. This provides all the more reason for us to reflect on power and politics while standing under Scripture.

### *Politics of Ministry*

"Politics is the art of getting things done with others."[2] It also includes the capacity to act and to influence others. How do "politics of ministry"[3] work in your ecosystem? What are the ways you work with others—deciding things, doing projects, presenting content, etc.? "Politics" is the term for navigating the relationships and interests involved in group work. Many of us grew up hating group projects in school—in junior high, figuring out my social status was tricky enough without adding to the mix the pressure of a grade decided in a group ecosystem. Working in an organization involves far more group projects than I had any clue about as a kid—somebody should have warned us.

The friction in any group project comes when competing interests, or even competing ways to obtain a shared interest, come to the fore. Finding our way through requires that we understand the kinds of power we (and others) hold, as well as what we are trying to do together.

There are two main families of power in organizations: formal and relational.[4] Formal power is acknowledged through a position, through foundational documents (like constitutions or bylaws), or in some other public and legitimized recognition. The CEO of an organization holds significant formal power. Relational power arises through connections with others in the web of relationships. It's usually practiced in smaller groups rather than across large swaths of people (like in a country). Think about a midlevel position held by someone who has been part of the organization for a long time, knows everyone, and is liked by everyone. When you run into this person in the hallway, if after chatting you find yourself having been talked into doing something that you hadn't thought that you wanted to do—that's relational power.

Some ecosystems of organizations thrive on formal power that is wielded well; some organizations buckle when formal power is enacted as the means to get something done. Some ecosystems welcome the practice of relational power; some seem to be allergic to it. In any organization, both families of power are present, but recognizing which is more welcome and recognizing the situations in which each is needed is really important.

Once we figure out which type of power is needed in the situation, we need to discern the activities of that power.[5]

- First, we have to be attentive to how the notions and positions of power play out in a room. This might include asking about the organizational chart for the formal aspect, but also about the history of relationships for the relational aspect. It absolutely means observing personalities and how people treat each other—reading the air in the room.
- Second, naming the unique interests and perspectives people are coming with is really helpful. Asking about the main concerns of

the players is a great first step, as well as staying focused on that main thing. We must also extrapolate from what is said and unsaid. Looking at the stakeholders' history of engagement on the issue allows us to go deeper in our understanding. This can be a really complex task because people are complex!

- Third, the activities grow in complexity because we next begin the process of negotiating. This ideally happens out in the open, without "backroom" deals or hiding things under the rug, but rather inviting conversation about the mission and the whole of the organization. The success of this step depends on objectivity, understanding that my personhood is not diminished if I let go of things, so I can seek mutual agreement without attacking others. I can set my own reasonable boundaries should others attack.
- Finally, with eyes wide open, we absolutely must sort through the implications of our negotiated decisions (this normally happens concurrently with the negotiation, but it's important enough to be named separately). There may or may not be a final arbitrator in the process. What are the moral and ethical implications of the decisions being made? What are the unintentional results of the decisions—as far as we can tell? What does it look like to name and take responsibility for our decisions and the effect they will have on others?

Developing our political acumen is absolutely possible, even for people who believe they despise "politics." One of the best ways to develop ourselves involves something relatively simple: a plan. Specifically, when our plans consider the interests of all the stakeholders and how what is negotiated will reflect kingdom priorities, we come to the table better prepared to grow the organization and see it flourish.

Learning to see interests does not come naturally. It requires practicing our empathy, and it's also about seeing ecosystem connections that may be "underground" or hidden in some way. It means asking questions to ferret out what may be intentionally or unintentionally veiled. Assuming "face value" in relationships is only the start when understanding interests in an ecosystem.

Shared interests can come from unexpected places. Consider the sea anemone and the crab: crabs will often sidle up to poisonous anemones and poke them so that they attach to the crab's shell. The crab then cruises along with its own bodyguard attached. The anemone and the crab protect each other, and the anemone hitches a free ride as well. Both interests are served in this unexpected partnership. Similar relationships exist in organizations—not every relationship makes sense on the surface, but sometimes observing who has lunch together reveals unexpected connections. One of my closest friends at work and I have almost no overlap in oversight, but we've found that our personalities, ethnicities, and life experiences, which also have little overlap, allow us to provide insight for the other in exceptionally valuable ways. The skills she has are very different from my own, and I have learned much from her—she's the colleague who tells me if I have a crazy take on a situation. I trust her *because* of the different power and interests that we hold.

Everyone comes to the table with an array of interests that translate into their expectations for how things should go in the organization. Humans understandably cluster around similar interests, as well as promote and defend them. However, if we are not careful, that can be threatening to others. Navigating political interests works best when we negotiate through the varied interests in pursuit of greater and higher goals—kingdom priorities. Things change when I recognize who is on my team and realize that we can find shared goals—all that's left is to work backward through the means available since we have that common purpose. It's not easy work, but once we put political interests in the right place, it's not as daunting.

One caveat: the presence of varied interests and perspectives is not as threatening if we are in a space of trust built by thoughtful communication. It's the communication piece we usually are frustrated by—maybe there is not enough of it or we hear it in the wrong tone. Our capacity to communicate effectively, especially on issues related to politics and power, is one-dimensional if we haven't nurtured the relationship apart from the particular issue at hand. If I only ever stop by a colleague's desk when I need to talk them into joining me in my particular interest, there's no relational capital to fall back on when another issue arises and I'm left with obligating support based on positional authority alone (which may or may not actually work depending on the appeal processes in the organization). If, however, my colleagues are confident that I am rooting for them, that we ultimately want the same things, and they see I'm attentive to their needs and concerns, they go above and beyond in a beautifully gracious manner. This ought to be the case whether there is a significant positional power differential or not. It's simply loving my neighbor.

A quick review of the nomenclature related to interest and power might be helpful as we put together our plans to negotiate toward kingdom priorities. In situations where we come to the table with equal power and shared interests, that's the space of collaboration—where we easily see what we are working toward. If we have equal power but conflicting interests, that's the time to bargain—we try to persuade others that everyone giving something up is going to be worth it. Even if the interests are different, maybe there's something they want that I can provide. In spaces of shared interests but unequal power, we network. Think old-school Rolodexes—looking for that one person at a conference, or LinkedIn in its best iteration. Finally, what happens when there are conflicting interests and unequal power? This is the space where we have to come with energy and creativity, high levels of social intelligence, and the capacity to see what others miss to bring that vision to those who assume they have no need for it. It's hard work and tricky, but gratifying in the end. Being clear on which category I'm working in contributes to effectiveness in conversations.

### *Hospitality*

In contexts in which the ultimate shared interest is the kingdom of God, a beautiful thing happens when we not only come ready to negotiate our interests but also with a posture of hospitality, welcoming others to the table. Holding these two together is important—if our convictions are legitimate, we cannot let go of the interests they represent. If we are kingdom citizens, we must embody the hospitality of the triune God wherever we are.

Even before we come to the table, we must be fully convinced that, as Josh Jipp notes, "We are God's guests and friends."[6] When we know we have been welcomed as friends, and that we are sitting across from another whom God has welcomed as friend, our posture must change. Christine Pohl describes this as how, "in hospitality we respond to the welcome God has offered and replicate that welcome in the world."[7]

Rebecca Hernandez offers a beautiful image illuminating where and how this goal of shared work takes place. Often undergirding our concept of hospitality is the "guest-host" model, where one party belongs and another is brought to the host's space, introducing another layer of power imbalance. I've been talking about "coming to the table" for negotiating interests, but I'd like to borrow from Dr. Hernandez and expand this table notion, as she does. She describes a vision of hospitality where we all live in the same shared house, with our own rooms as well as communal space.[8] This is "a big, big house with lots and lots of rooms,"[9] rather than a guest-host model. This allows us to appreciate the cultures, differences, and personalities of others. The paradigm she describes changes the dynamics of politics—getting things done together is less hierarchical and more purpose-focused. Power is less about control and more about cultivating a certain kind of space together. We have our own rooms, but in this house we inhabit together, coming to the kitchen table to talk through our differences is a unique experience, one that calls forth an eschatological vision.

### *Tool Kit: Constructing Conversations*

Given the complexity of coordinating people and plans related to conflict, a process for constructing conversations as a means of negotiating shared interests is the topic of this tool kit. We need conversations that move us somewhere in conflict mediation, or in just everyday working together. Reflecting on how to prepare for and approach these chats allows us to lower potential anxiety and genuinely welcome the other person to the shared table in our house. The challenge is that we don't all communicate in the same way, nor do we have the same assumptions about helpful communication. Collaborative communication requires the skills of adaptability and creativity, as well as a posture of humility and care.

Suppose you and several others have seemingly conflicting interests related to shared work, and things have gotten contentious. How could you coordinate things to address present conflict and change the tenor of the partnership? Here are a series of steps to work through:

1. The first task is to name the goal for all of you.
2. Next, identify what is important to each person—what are the interests and concerns present? Inviting the Spirit of God to illuminate what in you may impede the goals, what refining in you may need to happen, if there is sin, and how to better love your neighbor is always a helpful step.
3. Allowing people time and space to express what is important to them may need to happen with just the mediator rather than in the whole group, depending on the level of anxiety and conflict when everyone is gathered. Often having this conversation on someone's home turf (such as their office or an off-site neutral space) is helpful. Giving voice to this before the "real" meeting allows for people's thoughts to percolate. Sometimes then they can better explain the heart of the matter in the next conversation. Often our ears are better attuned to our emotions in these meetings, which I find to be the time when I can follow the Spirit's nudgings more closely and easily.
4. When the "real" meeting happens, more structure is usually better than less structure. That could take the form of a prepared agenda

sent out a couple of days ahead of time, or it could be just very clearly naming the purpose of the meeting and the means you all will agree on to reach that purpose as you talk. Sometimes naming the ground rules is necessary, but hopefully there's a level of professionalism that makes doing so irrelevant.

5. Progressing through the structure is the next step. Rigidity may not always be helpful if a participant figures out a better way to get to where you need to go. Remember that being clear on the problem is the foundation, not the way the solution needs to be reached. Space for creativity should always be welcomed.
6. Clear communication on next steps is important, as is accountability.
7. As appropriate, have all parties reflect on what the meeting meant in order for everyone to leave on the same page.
8. Following up to check on how people are processing the meeting builds relationships so that in future conversations, there is more trust present. Things are not concluded when you stand up from the table, but rather when you celebrate the problem's resolution.

The goal of these kinds of conversations, along with all the coordinating when there's conflict, is the same as expressed in Acts 6: that the word of God would continue to speak, that the number of disciples would increase greatly, and that those who are most unlikely to become obedient to the faith would find themselves so entranced by the way our ecosystems function, they cannot help but find out more. That kind of hospitality and stewardship of power changes everything.

### *Questions for Reflection*

1. How do you normally describe uneven power dynamics in your context? What stories do you tell yourself about your own power?
2. How do we use our power and time to best understand the interests of those with less power? Of those who don't have a seat at the table?

3. As you think about the kinds of group decisions made in your organization, which of the four activities of power are easiest for your group to practice, and which need more attention?
4. What does stewarding power in light of biblical hospitality look like in your context?
5. What are some hospitable practices and rhythms you can incorporate into your life and ministry?

# Part 2

## *Cultivation*

Ecosystems are intriguing because of their complexity.

Ecosystems are also frustrating because of their complexity.

Those entrusted with tending an ecosystem need a unique steadiness and insight into what is currently present, what needs to grow, and what needs to be pruned. This section is all about cultivation—the process of developing qualities or, in the vernacular, curating the vibe—of the organization. We will examine the place of artifacts in culture making, look at hospitable administration as a model for team development, and finally think about presence as a steadying and forward-moving means by which to cultivate the organizational ecosystem. As much as the topics of this section tend toward the conceptual, the tool kits are the stuff of our everyday—writing communications, leading meetings, and working with volunteers.

Let's begin with a scriptural word about wisdom. Complexity requires a lot of it! In complexity we find ourselves in the place we ought to start from—a posture of faith, trusting that the Lord sees the inner workings and relationships, the needs and the hopes of every participant in the ecosystem. He is our Creator and therefore is the expert Cultivator.

But what is it that he invites us into? James 1:5–8 helps us answer that: "[5]But if anyone is deficient in wisdom, he should ask God, who gives to all generously and without reprimand, and it will be given to him. [6]But he must ask in faith without doubting, for the one who doubts is like a wave of the sea, blown and tossed around by the wind. [7]For that person must not suppose that he will receive anything from the Lord, [8]since he is a double-minded individual, unstable in all his ways." The exhortation is clear: wisdom is missing, so it must be requested. Verse 5 is James's first mention of wisdom—he assumes his readers are familiar with the topic since he does not define it for them here. Broadly speaking, his readers would have understood wisdom from an Old Testament perspective—as a way of living, the path of following Yahweh in practiced obedience.

The request for wisdom is contingent upon not doubting. In this context, it seems like doubt could arise from questioning that God is able and willing to provide what is needed. So, if wisdom is practiced obedience, then doubt could be described as *procrastinating obedience*—a synonym for that is "disobedience." We who know the biblical witness of who God is and what God can do can become doubters when we do not practice the "knowledge" we have.

Let's parse out why we may be lacking in this area. For the sake of talking through something concrete (and normally stress inducing), let's use the example of being in a season of transition. Suppose you recognize the challenges of this, so you've asked God for wisdom on how to navigate the demands on your time and priorities in the transition. What are some of the reasons doubts could be present for us?

1. Perhaps we are prone to question something about God's abilities—is he actually able to give what the situation requires? Maybe this is a question of trusting the sufficiency of God's power, or the aptness of God using his power for what we want.

   *Regarding our scenario about praying for help with transition, maybe you are wondering if God is really able to move what seems immovable, to provide peace in the middle of the storm, to provide you with exactly what is needed in the chaos. Maybe you are even questioning if it is appropriate to expect him to do so.*

2. Perhaps we are not sure that the wisdom we need will come at the time it is required. It's getting down to the wire, and there's no help in sight.

   *Given our example, maybe it's Sunday night, and you can feel your anxiety rising as you look at your calendar for the week. There's so much to be done, and you don't know how to move forward on what you have to do because you feel stuck and without direction. How in the world are you going to find the time to do what you need to do, let alone do what you want to do? What if God doesn't answer your desperate prayer until next week, or next month, or next year?*

3. Perhaps we are prone to question that even if God does give us the right thing at the right time, we may miss it. God has a history of giving wisdom in unpredictable ways.

   *What if, in being distracted by your transition, you walk right by the person you should have chatted with, and in that conversation they would have provided you some illumination and encouragement, but you were so focused on the next item on your to-do list that you missed what God provided?*

4. Perhaps we question that the thing that comes at the right time and in the right way is actually the wrong thing. In other words, what if we are unwilling to act on the wisdom God has given? What if, as it turns out, we and the Lord are not on the same page about what kind of wisdom is necessary for transformation? What if what God wants to give us is not what we want to receive from him? What if our ideas for what the situation requires aren't ideas that will actually further the kingdom or glorify the King?

*In our example, what if, instead of being so focused on your uncertainty, you are being called to build a discerning spirit, and you need to learn that saying yes to one thing is saying no to another thing, but you think you can do it all? What if you've taken ownership of your time and your decisions, but God is calling you to remember that he owns all of that and you are a steward?*

Let's remember the context of this letter: James is writing to scattered tribes (1:1)—Jewish Christians who have left home base and are figuring out what it means to be away from what is familiar. This was also a community that probably experienced a number of tensions. Given James's exhortation relating to how they are to speak with and treat each other as the church, things were pretty rough among them. This is not a settled, utopian society that James is addressing. Being "scattered" is a particularly challenging state to be in—physically, mentally, and emotionally.

When we are scattered, we miss the thing that binds us.
Wisdom is knowing what or who our center is.
When we are scattered, it's a cross-cultural, uncomfortable experience from which emerges a cacophony of influences.
Wisdom is practiced obedience in the way of the Lord.
When we are scattered and cognizant of the trials present, we need something to hold on to in the midst of the chaos.
Wisdom is the anchor in the storm.

James does not describe this request for wisdom as haphazard or as an afterthought in a tough spot. It's a sincere and deep request that arises out of a recognition of our need. And there is a warning present—if we do not ask in faith, with the intention of living out what the Lord has given in answer to our request for wisdom, then we should not expect to receive it.

The picture of disbelief and distrust in James is so vivid: the instability of a wave in the ocean, the lack of steadfastness, constantly vacillating. This state of being is what one who is scattered must constantly guard against. For those in liminal space—after something has been left behind but before the new identity has been fully adopted—there is danger in succumbing to the temptation of not holding fast in faith and obedience.

When we are scattered and in liminal space, faith is either proved or destroyed.

As we continue this section looking at culture and change, God's message to us through James is vital. It's so easy to be overwhelmed by the complexity of what is going on—we must walk by faith or we will drown! He will provide exactly what we need when we need it.

# The Stuff of Cultivation

Suppose an organization purchases a software program as part of a cost-cutting initiative that will facilitate building usage. The software eliminates the danger of double booking, generates a master calendar, and ensures that all the necessary support (setup, food, cleanup) is centrally requested. That seems like a really helpful tool for the organization. However, what if, as part of that process, the "face" of the organization is removed, and automated emails are the primary means of communication going forward? What if the person who previously did the room reservations embodied the values of the organization on an expert level? What happens to the organization as a whole when that is suddenly gone? What if this software change ends up being a major factor in mission drift and no one realizes the culprit until five years down the road?

The examples of what happens to a natural ecosystem when humans intervene are myriad—sometimes something beneficial happens, sometimes something catastrophic happens, sometimes both. For good or ill, systems work the way we set them up to. Sometimes that ends up being exactly what we hope for, and sometimes the system produces an unintended consequence. This chapter is not about setting up a system that avoids these unintended negative consequences—it's practically impossible to do that given the complexity around us and our own limits. This chapter is instead about cultivating the "stuff" in our organizational ecosystems so that well-being and growth are all around us.

The goal of cultivation is to always contribute to the mission of the organization—that can be through direct ways or indirect ways.

For example, if the mission of a church has something to do with evangelism and discipleship, coupled with a focus on community, every participant should have a sense that what they are engaging in helps fulfill that mission, and that the "stuff" they have around them helps with that.

"Stuff" can be actual physical stuff, but it is also the words we choose as well as nonverbal communication. It's the air, dirt, and water in our garden metaphor. It's the art on the walls, the tone of the emails, the movement of bodies when greeting each other, and so much more. Sometimes visitors notice the air, the soil, and the water when they are wandering around a garden, but often what contributes to the garden flourishing is in the background, almost taken for granted unless we are looking for it.

### *Cultivation and Using Artifacts*

Andy Crouch says we make sense of the world by making something of it.[1] Therefore, to understand the world, we need to understand how specific artifacts—tangible cultural goods around us—fit into the story.[2] Crouch would have us ask the following questions about these artifacts:

1. What does this cultural artifact assume about the way the world is?
2. What does this cultural artifact assume about the way the world should be?
3. What does this cultural artifact make possible?
4. What does this cultural artifact make impossible?
5. What new forms of culture are created in response to this artifact?[3]

Let's walk through these five questions with some of my favorite artifacts found in my Anglican church. Our Sunday morning liturgy begins with a procession of three artifacts: a candle, a cross, and a copy of Scripture, each carried from the back of the church, through the sanctuary, to the front. They serve to remind us that the Holy

Spirit is among us, that we are a gospel people, and that we are here to be formed by the Word of God. When we reach the point in the service where the Gospel passage is to be read, those three artifacts are brought down from the platform to the middle of the room, where God's Word is opened and we hear about Jesus. It's a visual reminder that Christ, the Word of God, took on flesh and came among us, even as we are hearing the story of Jesus. I'm reminded of the incarnation every week—the beautiful truth that Jesus wants to be near me and that I can know him.

This section of the service assumes that we live in a forgetful world in which reminders of the nearness of God and the astounding nature of the gospel are needed on a regular basis. It assumes that if we lived in a world in which the gospel was even more at the forefront of our minds, we would be better off. What does this cultural artifact make possible? For me, it's grown my love of God's Word—both the Bible and Jesus, the Word made flesh—because both literally and figuratively I have learned to see in a new perspective. It's impossible for me to assume God is far-off or disinterested in the things of Earth because I observe that movement every week. What new forms of culture are created in response to this artifact? It strikes me as quite probable that the physical place from which we hear the gospel read has contributed to the location of our church potlucks. In our church, when we gather for a meal, often instead of eating at round tables in our pleasant but slightly dreary church basement, we set up a series of tables in the center aisle and across the front of the church for our meal. That image of us gathering around the Word during Sunday morning services has overflowed into the practice of us gathering as the body in that same sacred space to feast, to talk about the business of the church, as well as to hear about each other's lives. Jesus is what draws us together. I love that as we enjoy our monthly soup lunches after church, I am reminded of the incarnational nature of the gospel—how it changes strangers into family—all because of where my folding chair ended up.

In the busyness of our to-dos, it's easy to look past the artifacts around us. Often we feel like we don't have the time or energy to reflect on them. This chapter is a special invitation to pay attention. Think about what it's like to visit a new church—you notice details and make assumptions about things the regulars might not even see. Sometimes the meaning that is assumed to be attached to an artifact might astound us. What does it look like to ruthlessly communicate the meaning of "stuff" around us (and to be willing to adapt communication if incorrect assumptions continue to be made)?

### *Cultivation Values*

Crouch describes "cultivation" as making sure good things grow and flourish.[4] Our primary aim in cultivation is to keep in step with the Spirit of God. We can trust the Spirit's timing for growth. Whether for a large organizational change or a quick comment to a coworker about the tone of an email, keeping in step with the Spirit does not mean cultivation happens without challenge, but it does mean that we are seeking to walk humbly with the one who sustains all. When we value abiding with the Spirit, it changes how we walk through the ecosystem because we are not the prime mover; we are listeners, intent on staying with the Spirit.

The second value vital to integrate is that of love within cultivation. Whether it's going to Costco to get supplies for an event, rearranging tables at the last minute for a gathering, evaluating a budget plan, or taking out the trash, we cultivate out of love, obligation, or sometimes bitterness. We can also be tempted to cultivation as a performance, which is also lacking. In contrast, when those tasks are enacted from a posture of self-giving, for the good of others, love is present within the cultivation.

The final value for us to reflect on for creating culture is looking forward without ignoring the past or present. Developing the people around us for the future is vital cultivation work. Regardless of our position or authority, we all bear that mantle in an ecosystem. Crouch reminds us that we must engage in the disciplines of learning, paying attention, and studying history and context.[5] Even as cultivation is directed toward growth, those small acts of cultivation must make sense of the history and context of the organization. If a new event or program is to be introduced, we must justify how it is consistent with mission and history—ruthlessly. Especially in times of financial duress, the temptation is to come up with a myriad of options and see which one sticks—there are times when that works, but desperation can lead us to poorly made decisions.

Holding the past, the present, and the future wisely requires the kind of wisdom James describes, but it is more challenging to know when one of those needs to be emphasized above the others. Not every plant or organism in an ecosystem reaches maturation at the same time—this is also true for organizational ecosystems. Maybe newer members are more focused on the future because they haven't experienced perennial difficulties. Maybe older members only want to remember the "good old days" and ignore the blessings of the present. In any case, the administrative structures and processes may need to be couched in a way that past-, present-, and future-oriented people see their concern acknowledged as important. That takes patience and carefully reflected-upon communication (written communication is the tool-kit topic for this chapter).

### *Cultivation Tools*

Naming values is the easy part; the more challenging experience is building environments from those values. After looking at the unique set of tools environments require, we will explore the characteristics of an expert cultivator.

The foundational tool for cultivation is modeling—living those values out from a place of integrity with both confidence and gentleness. We can communicate beautiful integrity in our emails and in our hallway conversations, and we also live it when we have a tough day and the stress piles up. One of my personal values is to provide a nonanxious presence in the organizations of which I am a part. When I feel overwhelmed and the pressures compound, I have to notice my own emotional state and manage myself so that I do not overflow with irritability, or sarcasm, or snip at others, but rather I provide a patient and kind approach to whatever comes into my office.

Sometimes in an organization (versus a personal value as just described), another entity, like a board, senior pastor, or president, has responsibility for identifying values. If those named values are aspirational rather than actual, participants in the organization determine what to do with the gap. Do they choose to develop themselves along the lines determined, do they live with the disconnect, or do they find an organization with which they are better aligned? If a church names evangelism as a value of the community but leaders or members are not sharing the gospel, they need to figure out what to do with that disconnect. Each one of those choices could be the appropriate one depending on the situation—faithfulness is found in what one does in the waiting until the right choice emerges. Whether in the vulnerability of grappling toward growth, the graciousness of living with tension, or the generosity of leaving well, faithfulness and integrity are necessary.

Once a member of an ecosystem has adopted the values of the organization as a whole, the member is tempted to live as though people are dependent on the organization for the way those values are embodied. We want to imagine that we ourselves embody the meaning and mission, and we get stuck examining an exhibition of ourselves rather than our true selves. When pride creeps in, our authentic modeling crumbles so more harm than good is created. Sideways glances to notice who sees us remove us from the life we need to be living.

Cultivation is an endeavor of nuance. It is most commonly expressed in the language that we use, whether written or verbal. We rely on the denotation of expressions, and illuminate and illustrate connotations whenever needed. The right words open up worlds and communicate truth to all who have ears to hear. The wrong words constrict, set up boundaries, and lead to falsities. One phrase that I tend to use regularly is "I'm happy to . . . ," and it's almost always true that whatever task I'm agreeing to, or whatever news I'm delivering, my happiness is involved. I genuinely want the best for the person and the situation. However, every once in a while I find myself using that phrase when it's not true—I'm actually annoyed how the situation is progressing or I'm resentful the person is getting a positive response. Those moments of disingenuous cultivation are unhealthy for me and for the system. I have not cultivated well in my use of language because my expression was not truthful.

One of the most powerful language tools is the metaphor—an image that the entire community grasps that transcends simple description. Metaphors help us grasp problems, help us envision where we are going next, and offer clarity in complex times. Sometimes we talk about organizations as machines, a body, a family, a circus, or even an ecosystem! Choosing an accurately aspirational metaphor gives the opportunity to effect change. Images help us better connect over our shared experiences and find ways to adapt more easily.

Cultivation happens bilaterally—with authority from the top down and influences from the grassroots. Being in the middle, nurturing each at the right time and in the right way, allows for catalytic growth. Sometimes those in authority need feedback or a green light from others to enact their positional authority at the appropriate time. It can be a kindness to let a supervisor know that holding a boundary is needed even when there is pushback. Sometimes those without position need open doors or nudges to use the relational influence they have. Offering encouragement to team members to either share information or invite others to a coalition can be uniquely helpful. There are times when a senior leader cannot share information; however, others in the organization may be able to communicate freely, and that can be a significant help in cultivation. Knowing whose turn it is to listen and whose turn it is to act takes attentive listening.

In cultivation, we should keep the most important thing the most important thing. The vision that is woven throughout the organization that motivates our sweat, stress, and pain is ultimately our hope. Holding on to this hope ensures that our cultivation leads to unity because we see the vision enacted.

### *Cultivators*

What kind of people do we need to be for the right kind of cultivation to thrive? How do we get there? Crouch describes a posture as "our learned but unconscious default position, our natural stance. It is the position our body assumes when we are not paying attention." He says postures are the result of gestures (small actions) that, when put together, become habit.[6] This could be something as simple as smiling and greeting every person we see in the hallway; a habit like that affects our character and reputation. After we assent to the values and engage the tools, with time and practice, our posture becomes that of a "natural" cultivator. We edit ourselves and refine our use of tools, continually adapting our posture. Cultivating becomes a graceful movement, part of who we are as people. Instead of simply doing the action of smiling and saying hello, we have adapted to become a genuinely friendly person. This is why existing in an ecosystem with values contrary to our own is so draining and uncomfortable—it requires constantly performing actions, not engaging naturally from our posture.

A common and insidious pathway to unhealthy cultivation is to leave anxiety unaddressed because, as it overflows, there are far-reaching consequences. Perhaps you've experienced this within yourself or observed it around you. Anxiety that is woven throughout a system will seep into the soil with unwelcome implications. For example, if my anxiety causes me either to try and do more than my job or to disengage and do less than my job, the entire ecosystem will be thrown out of whack. An ecosystem with people who hold a lot of anxiety is a big problem because chronic anxiety leads to lower social intelligence. We will end up having a more difficult time refining the culture because we are not seeing our own or others' emotional responses to things. Cultivators must bring peace and gentleness as part of their nonanxious presence.

Our capacity for cultivation shifts negatively the more we live with anxiety. When we are hurried and busy, we skip the slow work of cultivation. Leaders need a lot of reflection time so that those nuances can be revealed. Keeping a short account with the Lord, confessing sin, and offering anxieties and burdens to him are crucial. That way, when we have an opportunity for exhortation or correction, we don't do it out of spite or anger. Our only motivation for those conversations ought to be care for the other person and for God's will to be done.

### *Tool Kit: Written Communication*

Words and images are the primary means of communication in our world, and, depending on the medium, one or the other is often emphasized. In a sermon comprised of words, the image of the speaker is present, as are verbal descriptions of concepts in the form of images. Social media uses an ever-adjusting approach to both—depending on the platform or your algorithm, you might be provided one over the other. In organizations, the foundation is often written words in the form of emails or messages. Gone for the most part are organization-wide memos.

Simple things make written communication successful: not sending something when irritated, reading things over multiple times to ensure meaning is appropriately communicated, considering the frequency of our missives, etc. The best thing to foster for this is empathy, or mindfulness of others. What would it be like to receive this message? So often our primary (if unacknowledged) motivation for written communication is "What will this do for me?"—to get something off my plate or get a task done the way I want it done, for example. What if, instead, the first thought as we write something is "How will my reader receive this?" We might find a more effective reception and therefore better outcome as we send it. If we continuously ask how this written thing will serve others, we put ourselves in a posture of honoring them.

Below are two examples of emails, one with inappropriate information and empathy, one that is corrected and holds a different tone. Sadly, the first one was sent and the second one was what I wish would have been written.

*Good morning,*

*Thanks for your help with the flyer. However, I need to insist that we include the information I gave you. If you think it too wordy, I'll deliver the flyer myself to every office instead of posting it.*

*One more thing to add: I had an argument with my condo management office the other day. The way they talked and acted showed that they were too full of their own authority. They had forgotten that their main job is to support the residents. Why am I reminded of them now? Do you really think I developed those flyers without any thinking?*

*Best,*
*X*

*Good morning,*

*Thanks for your help with the flyer. I appreciate your time and expertise that you generously provided to help me develop it. As one new to the organization and to planning events, your help is invaluable to me as I'm adjusting to this culture.*

*I wonder if you could help me understand more about why you suggested removing some of the information for this format. My thought was that the information would serve the community since this is a new event we are trying out. I would really appreciate learning more. Perhaps I could come up with some additional options for communicating the information in multiple formats as well? If you have any suggestions for that as well, that would be welcome.*

*Thank you again for your help.*

*Best,*
*X*

After receiving the first email, I invited "X" to have a conversation, which I'm grateful was productive as I heard about her frustrations due to some assumptions she made and I did not realize were present.

If I had known, I would have corrected them sooner. I'm hopeful that we have a good foundation for communication going forward.

When an organizational culture adopts this practice of writing to promote understanding, it's much easier to read to understand as well. Then, moving to the next step of speaking to serve is simple. An entire system like this is a breath of fresh air and a delight to be part of.

### *Questions for Reflection*

1. In what small acts of cultivation are you currently engaging? What could be some areas of cultivation for you to direct your energies toward?
2. Which tools of cultivation (modeling, nuance, bilateral listening) are you most comfortable with? Which do you want to grow in?
3. If there is a particular value you care about (either personally or organizationally), how could you plan to cultivate that value in the future?
4. Think about an example in which your written communication was effective—what about it made that so? Has there been an email that caused problems for you or your organization? What caused it to not accomplish what you expected it to?

5

# Hospitable Administration

In one of the most surprising moves in all of Scripture, the God of all knowledge, power, and creativity invited some ill-equipped and often disappointing ragtags to be his alpha team for changing the world. We know them as "disciples," and the world was transformed through them. We can replicate this act of divine hospitality (to a much lesser extent) by welcoming others into our organizations, responding to the grace God has shown in partnering with us. The core movement of hospitality is a transformation from stranger to "friend." Strangers are without a place, disconnected from life-giving relationships, but our organizations are strengthened when people are warmly welcomed into becoming "friend."

A particular quality of relationship accompanies this transformation of strangers to "one of us." Restaurateur Will Guidara has invited us into what he calls "*unreasonable hospitality*"—being "intentional and creative in pursuit of relationships." His intuition is, humans want to be taken care of because we experience something special when the right person takes care *of* us and takes care *around* us. Guidara describes this kind of hospitality as "the remarkable power of giving people more than they expect."[1] One night at Guidara's fine dining and eventually Michelin-starred restaurant, some first-time visitors to New York came to enjoy a meal. They casually mentioned to their server that the one thing they had not found the opportunity for during their New York visit was the experience of eating a hot dog from a street vendor. Guidara heard this and immediately went out, procured some hot dogs from the corner, and served them to the guests as one of their courses. Can you imagine them telling that story at home? Being seen and cared for with that small detail was creative, unexpected, simple, and full of meaning.

Stewarding the people and processes around us, facilitating that move from "stranger" to "friend" along the way, with intentional and creative pursuit of relationships *is* taking good care. We can choose to engage with others kindly and competently, yet at arm's length in that stewardship. Our parishioners, students, or customers might consider that to be sufficient. However, if the "stranger" into "us" transformation is filled with unreasonable care, this changes everything in the ecosystem. When we add the dynamic of surprising and delightful care, hospitable administration catalyzes directly to the heart of the organization. This kind of shift is not cosmetic—it's costly and vulnerable, and requires courage.

Beyond the benefit of surprising and delighting others, hospitable administration allows for unique expansion in the capacity of the organizational ecosystem. Think about the family who visited Guidara's restaurant—you can bet from then on they encouraged everyone they met to make experiencing a meal at Eleven Madison Park a top priority. Suddenly, the restaurant has evangelists from all over the city and the world touting the incredible experience of dining there. The diners are now part of the marketing team, insiders to the way this organization sees the world. Beyond that, I've never been to Eleven Madison Park, having only read Guidara's book,[2] but now I'm expanding the reach of the concept of "unreasonable hospitality" here. Our organizations can function similarly, although we will probably fail if our purpose behind hospitable administration is primarily for the growth of the organization. People detect self-serving motives like that quite easily.

Some sizes of organizational ecosystems may make it more difficult to practice hospitable administration than others. Just because a system is large or needs more automation does not mean this value cannot be expressed. Intentionality and creativity in relationships can still be present. Just because a system is small in scale does not mean the hospitality is automatically present—thoughtlessness happens everywhere.

How do we think about hospitable administration in light of community? We want people to know they belong. Those who have a strong internal sense of belonging to an organization are slow to leave, and their formation significantly changes with that sense. It's about moving together. We want people to share their gifts and to offer help, along with friendship. We want people to be valued and to understand they are part of the same body, with the same head. We want people to meaningfully contribute to the work of the organization.

### *Practicing Hospitable Administration in an Overwhelming World*

Hospitality best happens in the context of community because work is shared, so deeper rest is possible. The blessings of shared work are also deeper *because* they are shared. When hospitality is a hallmark of administration, we engage in boundary spanning, or bilateral relationship development, inside and outside the organization, drawing stakeholders into the work. Rebecca Hernandez, a higher education administrator for many years, has provided a helpful metaphor for hospitable administration. She observes that "the idea of a world house is a strong model for diversity in higher education. A big house where we live together, where we 'work out' our nuanced and not-so-nuanced differences to create a new culture that is large enough for the 'other' to become 'us.'"[3] This metaphor offers a captivating ideal for us to work toward, even in the complications of our context. Let's look at hospitable administration in light of three current significant issues in our world. While certainly much more could (and should) be said about these particular topics, what follows is a brief comment on how hospitable administration contributes to navigating these complexities, and I invite further reflection on how it could speak to other issues as well.

#### Polarizing Politics

Our world is seemingly obsessed with figuring out who is in and who is out, and political affiliation offers a means to provide identification that staunchly expresses those boundaries, sometimes to the point of demonization. While some organizations have clear lines about who belongs based on political affiliation, many do not. How can an organization facilitate a sense of belonging regardless of political affiliation? The primary starting point is to name the organization's assumptions about political belonging. What language or patterns of life are presumed regarding worldview, particularly relating to codes of ethics and morality, that potential members would need to understand? Once those are identified, removing the language from circulation provides clarity to understanding the organization's mission. If an outsider enters a church service, for example, and language about what "we all think" about a topic is changed into "here is what I think, why I think so, and let's talk about it," the outsider is invited to engage, not self-select into or out of the group. The posture of that first step is what sets the tone for one's trajectory. Hospitable administration in light of polarizing politics invites engagement, not bounded exclusion around secondary issues.

### Developing Technology/Artificial Intelligence

At first glance, technology, and especially artificial intelligence (AI), can seem antithetical to hospitable administration. However, like any tool, it can be used wisely for missional goals or irresponsibly and harmfully. Keeping our mission and values foremost as we discern technology usage is important, especially in the exploration phase when we are more likely to be tempted to use technology to make things easier or to help us with automation. Those are great goals and serve us and our systems well, but only if they are engineered to allow us to still enact our processes hospitably. AI can help us with forms, data, analysis, and so much more to effectively use our time and understand the experience of our stakeholders really well, so long as we maintain what is most important. Hospitable administration in light of developing technology is critically employing tools to create space for organizations to better do what they mean to do.

## Generational Gaps

In multigenerational organizations, gaps in understanding often occur along generational lines—the old guard is unaware of the needs of the younger people joining, the new folks gloss over the history, and the people in the middle bear the burden of keeping the organization going without much recognition from anyone. Generational gaps hold the opportunity for "intentionality and creativity in relationship"—that is, unreasonable hospitality. Listening to and sharing in the experience of another generation in our ecosystem can build our own capacity for cultivating a flourishing space. Sometimes we find the idea of a multigenerational community appealing, but not the practical outworking. In my multigenerational church, not everyone always connects with the song we are singing, but we know that someone in the room does. Sometimes the babies interrupt, but we have prayed for children to join us, so we all smile when we hear them, especially at those inopportune moments. Sometimes we have to plan for the older folks who do not drive at night or make sure they are safe going down the stairs to the church basement. When I see how this community greets each other on a Sunday morning, all of that is, of course, so worth it. Hospitable administration in light of generational gaps is empathy directed toward greater enlightenment of the organizational ecosystem.

## *Formative Aspects to Hospitable Administration*

It takes both a certain way of thinking and a certain way of being to practice hospitable administration. In my experience, the following five practices contribute to hospitable administration.

First: *be prayerful.* One of the greatest blessings about working in an organization is that, as we engage with people, there is a significant potential for a ripple effect. We never know how a relationship will continue and develop when someone departs an organization. We never know what one point in a sermon will mean to someone or how one conversation will shape the trajectory of someone's life. Abiding in Christ, always listening to the Spirit, is the best way to ensure we are partnering with the Lord in what he wants to do in the world. Pray boldly. Pray specifically. We should expect God will use us. The potential is staggering.

This book is a tangible outflowing of a ripple effect in my life. When I was doing my master's degree, my friend Bill suggested I read an article about pastoral imagination. He was right—I thought it was a fascinating topic, and the concept stuck with me.[4] After I graduated and served in a local church, I eventually ended up working in higher education administration. A major focus of my PhD reading and research was formation in the context of theological education, since my full-time job was in student life. I remembered the Dykstra article from nine or so years previously and reread it. That description of imagination sparked my thinking, eventually leading me to my dissertation topic: administrative imagination. Having thought a lot about administration and its life-giving potential, I thought a book on the topic could serve the kingdom of God. Here we are, all because Bill mentioned an article to me. God's economy is astounding—all we have to do is follow his nudging.

Second: *be present.* Hospitable administration requires our whole, authentic selves. Not just our emails or our phone calls, nor evidence that we were in the office, but our warm and welcoming presence. It's greeting others kindly in the hallway. It's caring when someone seems to be having a difficult day. Sometimes being present for even the smallest moments ends up carrying significant meaning. At my institution we ask graduates to identify the three most important influences on their educational experiences—"interactions with students" is the top-rated item. As students process through their learning with each other, formation happens and fruit is born. Most schools have the same data point—and it is the same for both in-person and online education. Proper presence in service to hospitable administration fosters opportunities for meaningful engagement, increasing the likelihood that strangers will become one of us.

Third: *be sticky*. "Create connections," in Guidara's words. The social dynamics in our communities are varied. There are so many types of people in our ecosystems: introverts, people with anxiety, people who are insecure, busy people, people with addictions to social media, and so much more. We need sticky skin because connections create meaning. This means engaging in familiar chitchat that often sounds like the "who do we both know" game, having the "what do we both like to do" conversation and the "this is what our shared experience was like for me" chat. Try to stick with people—with invitations, with conversations, etc. We also need thick skin because we might get rejected. We need to be okay if someone's response is "no, not this time" and not assume we know the reason for the rejection. We should pay attention to social cues, develop our social intelligence, and invite stickiness.

Fourth: *be generous*. Guidara calls this "the remarkable power of giving people more than they expect." Budgets get cut all the time, and sometimes our ideas for generosity cannot be responsibly funded by our organization. Generosity doesn't always mean spending money, nor does it mean funding organizational initiatives with personal money. It does not mean living without wise and healthy boundaries. However, it does require us to pay attention to the Spirit and prayerfully be ready to offer what the Lord invites us to—that might be time, conversation, encouragement, or something else. When we are stressed, we have a choice to walk with a spirit of generosity or a spirit of restriction. It's best to choose now what our posture will be later.

Fifth: *be imaginative*. This is the culmination of the other four: *Our prayer, presence, stickiness, and generosity, woven together, lead us to imaginative action that creates the experience of unreasonable hospitality.* I have so many wonderful examples of this in my life, but one of my favorites is something a former coworker used to do. When I was away on vacation, he would often sneak into my office and hide something small for me to find. One year I came back from Christmas break to a picture of a mouse underneath my computer mouse.

I've returned from a long weekend to a plastic but very real looking roach on my desk. And, every once in a while, a piece of dark chocolate would show up—you can guess which item I preferred. I think Jason was equally pleased whether I smiled or was startled. He knew that I love a good practical joke. This mischief was an imaginative expression of hospitality because it made coming back to work more fun. I felt welcomed back to work when it was sad to leave my family and friends.

### *The Shunammite Woman*

The Shunammite woman we read about in 2 Kings is an example of unreasonable hospitality in Scripture. Second Kings 4:8 notes that she "insisted" that the prophet Elisha come for a meal at her house, and that created a tradition—whenever he passed that way, Elisha visited this family. That's already quite hospitable of this woman. She also talked her husband into building a guest room for Elisha (2 Kings 4:10). In gratitude, Elisha asks what he can do for her. She's quite content with her life, and she doesn't even ask for the most significant thing she and her husband are missing—a child. She's just happy to walk with Elisha in a very generous and practical way. It seems quite reasonable to infer from this passage that she prayed about her acts of hospitality in giving Elisha a comfortable and restful space. She and her husband had already offered their presence by inviting him for meals. We read about the stickiness of "insisting" that he come over. This was a generous thing to do, and the "imaginative" practice comes in a very sensible sort of way. A guest room in a world without Ikea or Amazon would include only the very basics, but the passage specifies that they built a space with not only a bed but a "table, chair and lamp." The Shunammite woman went beyond the very essential furniture (just a bed) and designed and cultivated a space for Elisha to work and prepare for ministry with a table, chair, and lamp. This woman had a vision for Elisha's ministry and an empathetic understanding of his experience, anticipating his needs. Then, she built it for him. That's imagination come to life in the form of unreasonable hospitality. What a beautiful illustration of what hospitable administration can contribute to God's work in the world—welcome, connection, vision, and practical expression.

### *Tool Kit: Saying Yes Until You Have to Say No*

The tool for this chapter is unique from others in that, instead of a skill or practice, it is about adopting a mind-set—an automatic assumption that comes prior to the expression of a particular skill. Simply: *say yes until you have to say no*. In an attempt to be hospitable, having this as our go-to answer allows for both our own hospitable action and our organization's capacity to be ready for action. We are building a natural bias toward action with this mind-set, facilitating movement and energy. It's about openness to new ideas and opportunities. We are more likely to try things out because our stance is ready for movement. Years ago I asked an innovative leader how she engages herself and her coworkers so that the programs and projects she cares about can happen given all the frustrations of institutional life. She said she says yes until she has to say no. As I've incorporated that into my life, and started seeing it in others as well, I'm convinced that simple approach leads to catalytic results.

Before we adopt the automatic decision to say yes, though, we need to know when to say no. That means attentiveness to our energy and capacity, our convictions and ethical guidelines, as well as other boundaries. Boundaries should be adaptable depending on variables. For instance, in a really busy month it might be helpful to think through what would warrant you staying an extra thirty minutes at work to get a few more things done when you might not choose to do so in a less busy month. Moving boundaries in a healthy way means we have agency and therefore freedom and choice in moving them. Owning our no requires reflection and practice—paying attention when something feels off, as well as acknowledging how others and the organization may be affected by our no. Sometimes we are tempted to set boundaries after receiving a negative response in an experience; however, prayerfully bringing that painful situation to God so he can direct our future plans is vital.

Once our reasons for saying no are clear to us, then we have the simple yet incredibly difficult opportunity to teach ourselves to not second-guess our clear yes. Developing this new pattern of thinking takes time and training. Practically, that means:

- Naming what is currently prohibiting us from saying yes until we have to say no. Is it fear? Laziness? Already feeling too busy?
- Ensuring that this new mind-set is at the forefront of our minds (maybe we actually have this phrase on a sticky note at our desk!).
- Noticing our natural yes so that we can identify that feeling in the future.
- Chatting with trusted colleagues and friends about their observations on how you practice this mind-set.
- Recognizing that mind-sets take time to develop roots, and when we act outside of this mind-set, it's worth paying attention to why that's happening.

It can feel nerve wracking and fear inducing to adopt this mind-set. It's worth trying out, though. Saying yes until we have to say no means we live out of freedom and openness, leading to joy and hope.

### *Questions for Reflection*

1. Have you had a formative experience of going from "stranger" to "friend" in a particular community? What did you observe about the challenges and blessings of that transformation?
2. When was a time you were "intentional and creative in pursuit of a relationship"? How was that received? How did you process that initiative?
3. Which of the three overwhelming aspects of hospitable administration do you tend to find most challenging (political polar-

ization, technology, or generational gap)? What is one small adjustment you could make in that area to further your hospitable administration?

4. Which of the five ways of pursuing hospitable administration is easiest for you (prayerful, present, sticky, generous, or imaginative)? Which is most difficult?
5. What gets in the way of you being a "say yes until you have to say no" person?

## 6

# Proper Presence

In an organizational ecosystem, each participant has some options about the vibe they want to personally pursue in that space. Will they be the one with a great sense of humor and is easy to be around? The one who thoughtfully gives everyone a birthday card? The one who oozes maximal efficiency? The one who listens to everyone's complaints with empathy? Even as we attempt to be genuinely ourselves in these administrative spaces, we also have the opportunity to engage the formative parts of ourselves, moving toward helpful models and examples. Exodus 33 is a beautiful meditation on the idea of presence and provides a helpful reflection on what it means to express our needs. It's a dialogue between Moses and Yahweh as Moses comes to grips with the task before him.

> [12]Moses said to the LORD, "See, you have been saying to me, 'Bring
> this people up,' but you have not let me know whom you will send
> with me. But you said, 'I know you by name, and also you have
> found favor in my sight.' [13]Now if I have found favor in your sight,
> show me your way, that I may know you, that I may continue to
> find favor in your sight. And see that this nation is your people."
>
> [14]And the LORD said, "My presence will go with you, and I
> will give you rest."
>
> [15]And Moses said to him, "If your presence does not go with us,
> do not take us up from here. [16]For how will it be known then that I
> have found favor in your sight, I and your people? Is it not by your

> going with us, so that we will be distinguished, I and your people,
> from all the people who are on the face of the earth?"
> [17]The LORD said to Moses, "I will do this thing also that you
> have requested, for you have found favor in my sight, and I know
> you by name."
> [18]And Moses said, "Show me your glory."
> [19]And the LORD said, "I will make all my goodness pass before
> your face, and I will proclaim the LORD by name before you; I will
> be gracious to whom I will be gracious; I will show mercy to whom
> I will show mercy." [20]But he added, "You cannot see my face, for
> no one can see me and live." [21]The LORD said, "Here is a place by
> me; you will station yourself on a rock. [22]When my glory passes
> by, I will put you in a cleft in the rock and will cover you with my
> hand while I pass by. [23]Then I will take away my hand, and you will
> see my back, but my face must not be seen." (Exodus 33:12–23)

Moses is in a really difficult place. His task is to rescue the Israelites from Egypt, but in his perception God has not given him what he needs to do this (v. 12). Moses knows where to go for help—he recognizes his dependence on the Lord to show him the way to do what seems impossible (v. 13). Moses has already bought into the project—he knows this is the right thing to be done—he's been advocating for the people to the Lord. Yahweh's response to this request is so simple: he will go with Moses. It's a straightforward response, laden with meaning and hope. Connected to that in this remarkable clause is "and I will give you rest."

Moses asks to see God's ways, but God gives himself. That's grace! It's God's presence that Moses most needs. Cognizance of God's ways is helpful but insufficient. We need all that God's presence brings with it. It's also worth noting that Moses's desire is to please God (v. 13), not to make the people happy or to get them there safely. His heart is rightly oriented. Moses didn't tell God he was tired and worn out. He didn't ask for rest, but this offer of rest was God's gracious response to Moses's need. In this passage, rest isn't something we demand or take; it's something that's given to us. When the Lord offers rest, it is as an assurance that we are always limited, always dependent on the Lord.

In verses 15–16 Moses realizes how right God is—everything depends on God going with them. After this exchange between Moses and God, the Lord offers Moses an experience that cements his commitment to the exodus about to take place. When Moses asks to see the Lord's presence, God responds that his goodness will pass before him. Moses is hidden in the cleft of the rock, covered by the Lord's hand, and sees a sight beyond compare.

This vignette offers us the opportunity to self-evaluate. We too can have confidence the Lord will give us himself. With that, of course, he always gives us the way to do our work. Are we like Moses in that our desire is foremost to please the Lord, or do other inclinations creep in? In a frantic and rushing world, a posture of readiness to receive rest from the Lord stands out. Let's also make sure we are attentive to the ways that the Lord is going with us and giving us his presence. Our proper presence is predicated by the Lord's presence.

### *Cultivation and Presence*

In this section we've been exploring what it means to be a cultivator in an organizational ecosystem in light of the essential work of administration: stewardship of people, resources, and projects through a process. This chapter will attend primarily to the person and postures of the administrator because of the primacy of our proper presence. It's insufficient to design a process or even a whole system that may function optimally but is devoid of our influence as image-bearers of God. The kind of organizational cultivation we strive for depends on the right kind of presence from its cultivators.

Presence comes in many forms, including digital presence, cognitive presence, emotional presence, social presence, of course divine presence, and more. Given both the factors that make up human beings and the tools we engage, we must pay attention to many things as we develop the facets of our presence. Different facets may be shown depending on the type of presence. How do we present ourselves via the medium of a screen, or even just through the medium of audio? How do we come across in a hallway conversation or in a one-to-one meeting? What do people experience in a large crowd when we communicate?

Let's start with a model of "practical inquiry" as a means of thinking through the logical steps of engaging with subject matter and build our concept of presence out from there.[1] The first step in human cognitive engagement is a triggering event—something incites a question or a kind of dissonance. Let's say you notice in a couple of conversations that people seem unusually stressed about attending your organization's events because they are so busy. So, you start wondering what that's all about, and you jump into the second step: exploration. Exploration often involves engagement with opportunities and people outside of our own minds—asking a colleague a question for their perspective or reading someone else's thoughts on the matter. In this example, maybe you start asking the leaders more specific questions about the logistics of their events and why they think attendance is down. Then (again, this is logical and ideal but may not happen sequentially like this in the real world) you can integrate what you've uncovered in the exploration phase and create meaning. Maybe you put together a few things and realize that this is a perfect storm of unrelated factors: a new kids' sports director for the county is changing up everything, a couple of small-group leaders are in their busy season at work, and the local high school spring play is claiming all the regular babysitters. The final phase is resolution, which requires action to address the instigating triggering event.[2] That final step is the world of administration—getting a problem solved. However, if we neglect the other three areas (triggering event, exploration, and meaning making), our solutions are curtailed. For our example, suppose there's a really important church leaders' meeting that needs to happen, so you put together all the data you have and switch it from its normal Thursday evening slot to early Saturday morning (before the kids' games, not during the workweek), breakfast and babysitting provided (and you pay those teenagers really well to incentivize them to get out of bed!), and it works! The authors of this model recognize this process as the foundational piece of cognitive presence—when something triggers us enough to get us to explore the matter, piece together the information, and then resolve the matter, we've engaged cognitively. That is necessary but insufficient for the kind of presence that cultivation requires. Our cognitive presence, in this example, allowed for a helpful plan.

Cultivation requires giving of the self for the good of the whole, which means the triggering event incurs a cost to be paid by the cultivator. Think of a farmer who wakes early in the morning to tend to his livestock, who, by toil and sweat, waters his crops and anxiously peers at the sky hoping for rain. There is a physical and psychological toll that he pays for this privilege of cultivation. He would never vacation during harvest or sleep in whenever he feels like it. He's sacrificed himself for the endeavor.

Theologian T. F. Torrance says self-sacrifice is the form Trinitarian love takes in a fallen world.[3] God the Father, Son, and Spirit exist in perfect love and communion outside of what happens in the created universe. When Jesus entered this space at a particular moment in time, the way that perfect love was expressed came in the form of him giving up his life for love. It's the same for us—whatever love of the Trinity exists in us because we have been adopted by the Father, united with Christ, and indwelt by the Spirit, can only be expressed in self-sacrifice. Our proper presence requires love that is willing to lay down our lives. Perhaps it is jarring to think about bringing that level of love to administration—it's not to say that an administrative task is worth dying over, but loving others, potentially through the work of administration, is the invitation Jesus gives us when he reminds us that no greater love exists than that we lay down our lives for our friends (John 15:13).

For administrators, the key concept of stewardship inherent in our cultivation is that we take good care of what has been entrusted to us. The way we do that requires at least four approaches to our stewardship: we need to be observant, unhurried, wondering, and nonanxious.

### *Observant*

A steward oblivious to what is going on is irresponsible—it's someone who holds a title but does not embody the role. An excellent steward cultivates the skill of observation. Some people may seem more naturally observant, but noticing is a skill we can develop, retraining our brains and our bodies. With intentionality we can slow down, not walking as quickly from one meeting to the next, living at a different pace that allows us to absorb more of what is going on around us. Intentionally engaging our senses, putting down our phones, and inviting others into a more experiential way of going through the world help us be more observant.

Being observant allows us to shift our gaze from what is right in front of us to what is off in the distance. It means being aware of what is happening on the periphery as well as what demands our attention right in front of our faces. It also means observing what is going on in our internal world. The skill of observation means absorbing words spoken as well as words unspoken. It also means organizing all that information into helpfully accessible categories to be available when we need it. Just like we file emails or documents into folders, we can do the same with information. It takes time and practice, but what initially takes awareness in organizing can eventually become intuitive or second nature.

I've worked in residence life for decades, and since I was nineteen, every August has brought a lovely onslaught of new people into my life whose stories, experiences, and current realities now need to be part of my engagement with them. From the fifteen women in my hall when I was their RA in college to the dozens of new students I orient to seminary every year, it's important to me that I remember the names, histories, and hopes of these students. In an ever-increasingly challenging task, I repeat names to myself when I walk away from conversations, I review housing lists, and I ask my coworkers to remind me about a person when I know I'm missing something vital. I've trained my brain to organize itself around mental filing cabinets. In my brain is a room full of cabinets that you yank open, find the right hanging folder, and then slot your paper into the right spot. I open the individual student's filing cabinet in my brain and put information in when it comes my way. (My favorite kind of information is when I look out my window and see a young man and a young woman heading out together to study or go on a walk—sometimes those individual files of students formally connect to each other because I find out they are engaged, and it's a delight.) There are certainly other mental models to engage—maybe younger administrators use a mental electronic folder system in their minds—but the idea is to organize our brains so information is stored in a place we can access it.

### *Unhurried*

Most of us live with the temptation of hurried busyness. We can pretty easily fill our days and calendars with seemingly important tasks, conversations, and projects. However, it's harder to be observant when our pace is (as my department administrative assistant calls it) "like a train schedule"—in and out every two minutes. Not all of us have the privilege of a work environment where we can say no to things because our agenda is often dictated by others. However, there are things that are in our control—especially the language we use and the posture we take. For example, I've stopped using the word "busy" when people ask me how I am doing, since almost everyone could say that and it's not helpful. However, often I *am* busy, so I've shifted my answer to "things feel full." I don't want to bury the stress of my reality, and it's important to offer an authentic look into how I actually feel at the moment. When I notice that things feel full, I can prioritize finding margin where possible, often negotiating with myself. I can keep my boundary of not checking email once I leave work, or I can choose to extend my boundary by doing some emailing in the evening or before I go to work so the next day at least begins less full than it would otherwise. Being busy and hurried feels stress inducing, but acknowledging the fullness of the season is validating the truth, which can lead to improved problem management.

### *Wondering*

Perhaps the most helpful word for the administrator seeking to be a wise and helpful cultivator is "wonder": as in, "I wonder what it means that . . ." or "I wonder how we might . . ." Instead of asserting our perspective on a matter, instead of imposing a structure, wonder creates possibilities. There is a difference between a supervisor walking into an office, saying, "Please fix this registration issue" and one saying, "I wonder if there are ways we can lower barriers of entry for participants." The posture of "wonder" allows us to play and explore in a manner that helps lower defenses and invites collaboration. It also more easily draws us to access our curiosity. This word ought not to be used as manipulation or puppet mastering of people, however, but out of our genuine exploration in trying to resolve a problem or issue. It's the difference between asking questions and giving answers, and sometimes the former changes the tone of everything because it opens conversations rather than closes them.

### *Nonanxious*

The final approach is offering a nonanxious presence to the ecosystem. Those with nonanxious presence help raise the emotional intelligence of the organization. Anxiety has a tendency to either make us less aware or heighten our senses to a state of hyperawareness, which can be distracting. A nonanxious presence contributes to facilitating an environment where everyone can more easily focus on the mission.

A metaphor for this type of presence is a "helmscope," which is a portmanteau word combining the idea of helmsman (the prime mover of a vessel, the person embodying the opportunity for action) with gyroscope, an apparatus that provides stability in change. Someone embodying a nonanxious presence helps provide vision for the journey as well as the know-how to steady the vessel when there are rough seas. An administrator who acts as a helmscope contributes to the organizational ecosystem's ability to weather the storm. Proper presence is indeed a "helmscope," giving the administrator eyes, ears, hands, and feet to live into the organization's mission and values, stewarding people, programs, and processes toward those ends. Proper presence offers a hopeful response to the many challenges facing organizations for the sake of the kingdom of God and his church.

### *Tool Kit: Managing Volunteers*

Many of our organizational ecosystems are composed of both paid employees and volunteers—those who give of their time and effort without compensation. A somewhat different skill set is needed for managing volunteers than for managing employees. We need to be sure we have the right category in mind for each group with whom we interact.

Volunteers are not getting a paycheck, so their loyalty to the organization is not dependent upon financial benefit. Many times people begin their engagement with an organization as volunteers as an inroad to connect to the mission or the larger body. Then they often develop deep community and connections. Sometimes the mission focus lessens through those relationships, sometimes it's emphasized.

Managing employees is different from managing volunteers—employees can be removed from the community, their financial situation may change, or future opportunities can be affected, etc. While the tone of how we communicate with volunteers and employees might not be significantly different, the power behind the communication makes all the difference in how the message is received.

Reliability and availability are the biggest frustrations in working with volunteers. Employees are supposed to work specific hours, and you can depend on them for that. Volunteers expect a flexible schedule and might not tell you ahead of time when the schedule you labored over will not work for them. But both volunteers and employees want to feel like they are doing meaningful work. A few years ago I discovered the word "voluntold"—and I try to use the concept behind it discerningly—which means informing volunteers what we *require* of them. Discerning what is worth making mandatory and what is invitational is important to keeping the appropriate level of engagement. Most volunteers are happy to be required to attend a reasonable amount of orientation and training, but they get bitter when flexibility is not present for when another priority pops up. And, of course, the tone in which someone is "voluntold" to do something is very important. Sometimes self-selection into an opportunity holds more power than a requirement.

Communication with volunteers is at its best when it includes regular reminders and cues toward the "why" of what we are doing at the organization. Volunteers normally have less engagement with the organization—it's one thing in the midst of many demands on their time and attention—so keeping the main thing the main thing is really important. Additionally, communication should help the volunteers appreciate and see what is going on in other parts of the ecosystem with which they may not regularly engage. Helping them see how what they do impacts other parts of the ecosystem is vital to the health of the whole.

I have a former coworker who has developed some of the most faithful and loyal volunteers I've ever encountered. Herb thinks very intentionally about mission and communication, striving to embody the mission of the organization in himself. He holds his volunteers to high standards of excellence and invites them into meaningful contributions. Herb can do that because his level of personal investment in the lives of his volunteers is high. He invites them into his life—I can't even count the number of barbeques held at Herb's house when we were doing ministry together. He also gently invites himself into their lives, shepherding his people with wisdom and grace along the way. When Herb moved to a new house, the whole moving crew was made up of his volunteer team—and they were glad to be there doing the laborious work because of Herb's history of being there for them. There's always laughter, and sometimes crying together—it's just doing life while welcoming volunteers into it. It's unreasonable hospitality in the form of proper presence in a very "come over and let's grill burgers on Friday" kind of way.

### *Questions for Reflection*

1. Given Moses's conversation with God in Exodus 33, is there anything you are missing related to how you think about your work?
2. What are the most challenging obstacles to your appropriate presence in your organization?
3. Think about a good experience you had as a volunteer, as well as a bad one. What made each experience so?
4. What is one thing you could do to offer more helpful presence to the volunteers with whom you work?

# Part 3

## *Fruitfulness and Dominion*

There's almost nothing more frustrating than investing time, energy, and money into something and then having to walk away with nothing to show for it. The cost is high, and we leave empty-handed. It's infuriating. One of the complexities of being part of God's economy (and by "economy" I mean the original meaning of the word in Greek—household management) is we function without the perspective or view that he holds. By faith we recognize we may never see or understand how the head of this household chooses to employ our efforts and resources. John 15:1–17 helps ground our expectations and our hopes about fruitfulness:

> "I am the true vine and my Father is the gardener. He takes away every branch that does not bear fruit in me. He prunes every branch that bears fruit so that it will bear more fruit. You are clean already because of the word that I have spoken to you. Remain in me, and I will remain in you. Just as the branch cannot bear fruit by itself, unless it remains in the vine, so neither can you unless you remain in me.
>
> "I am the vine; you are the branches. The one who remains in me—and I in him—bears much fruit, because apart from me you can accomplish nothing. If anyone does not remain in me, he is thrown out like a branch, and dries up; and

> such branches are gathered up and thrown into the fire, and are burned up. If you remain in me and my words remain in you, ask whatever you want, and it will be done for you. My Father is honored by this, that you bear much fruit and show that you are my disciples.
>
> "Just as the Father has loved me, I have also loved you; remain in my love. If you obey my commandments, you will remain in my love, just as I have obeyed my Father's commandments and remain in his love. I have told you these things so that my joy may be in you, and your joy may be complete. My commandment is this—to love one another just as I have loved you. No one has greater love than this—that one lays down his life for his friends. You are my friends if you do what I command you. I no longer call you slaves, because the slave does not understand what his master is doing. But I have called you friends, because I have revealed to you everything I heard from my Father. You did not choose me, but I chose you and appointed you to go and bear fruit, fruit that remains, so that whatever you ask the Father in my name he will give you. This I command you—to love one another."

The experience of fruitfulness is always deeply connected to Jesus. He deepens us in maturity as we progress in our goal of being like him, learning from him. Without being anchored to him, without being tethered with him, we will wither and die, fruitless, bitter, and ready to be destroyed.

We have been appointed, or directed, to bear fruit, but there are contingencies for this—we must remain *in* Jesus, loving others in order to bear this lasting fruit. As administrators, this assurance of what will last is comforting—in a world of distractions, short-term attention, and faulty memory, what comes from the Lord is starkly different. We must lean into that, praying for what *is* of the Lord to come about, and what *is not* to burn away like dead branches and dry leaves in a bonfire.

Given their complexity, ecosystems push us toward trusting the Master Gardener. We endeavor to provide care for what little we have stewardship over, but at the end of the season, we have little power over the quality of the fruit that is produced. Our power lies in our own choice to faithfully and lovingly enact our role. In this section we will explore the idea of fruitfulness, developing both practices that pull us toward that hope and postures that keep us connected to the vine.

7

# "Taking Good Care" Versus Dominion

There are myriad ways to take "bad care" of the people and processes for which we have responsibility. From abusers who actively seek degradation to those who simply (and irresponsibly) assume that something is taken care of without checking, there is a spectrum in how our stewardship is harmfully or unfaithfully expressed. Sadly, this has been part of the human story since the very beginning. In Genesis 3 we see the heartbreaking consequences of "bad care." The serpent, Adam, and Eve are each cursed in a way that curtails their fruitfulness on the earth. The serpent will crawl and be crushed. Eve will suffer in one instance of her fruitfulness (childbirth) and desire dominion but will not receive it. Adam will suffer in an expression of his fruitfulness (gardening) and will be defeated by death, which overtakes all humankind. Thus began a trajectory of agony, a struggle toward fruitfulness, and desperation stemming from corrupt relationships and scarce resources.

That trajectory was interrupted by Jesus's resurrection, which prevails against the curse in an "already/not yet" manner. Sin has been defeated, *and* wholeness has not come yet. While we wait for completion, we look to Revelation 21 to help us envision the instantiation of the complete reversal of the curse of death. In that culminating moment, all tears are gone, and death will not exist any more. The Garden City that we read about in Revelation will be filled with rivers, trees, streets, and homes into which God's people will enter and dwell, full of flourishing and fruitfulness. It is this gracious vision from the Gardener-Architect in which we delight.

### *Stewardship*

As a means of unpacking the concept of "taking care" more fully, let's explore the mantle, or responsibility, associated with stewardship. Perhaps your experience of air travel has included the same era as mine—where decades ago those whom we now refer to as "flight attendants" were designated "stewardesses" or "stewards." There were (and still are) two main aspects of that job: to ensure that passengers are safe and make certain their needs are provided for. In the context of an airplane, the most common provisions are seatbelts and snacks, but flight attendants are also trained to deal with extreme circumstances—doors that fall off in midair, agitated passengers, and much more.

In the context of administration, safety and provision can come in many forms. Ensuring safety might mean looking at a building's fire code, performing background checks, and addressing suspicious or manipulative behavior. Provision might be ensuring a group has paper plates or whiteboard markers, teachers are adequately trained, or communication to the community is clear and accessible. Stewardship means choosing to pick up the appropriate responsibility for the person, program, or process. Both adequate safety and provision are necessary for the ecosystem to flourish. When danger and scarcity are present, there is a strain on the system and fruitfulness is curtailed.[1]

*Appropriate* responsibility is a tricky thing. Some of us tend toward taking responsibility too early and for too much—that's overfunctioning. Some of us tend toward avoiding responsibility, so we come to it too late and for too little. Often our childhood experiences shape our tendencies—if our parents were less engaged, we may overfunction. If various family members overfunctioned, we may tend toward underfunctioning. "Right-functioning" may not be something everyone in an ecosystem agrees upon, so negotiating becomes vital to system fruitfulness. The right level of function is sometimes in the eye of the beholder. I once stepped into a system in which memory of my predecessor's predecessor was quite powerful because she was a prolific and influential overfunctioner—well loved and admired. My immediate predecessor concluded her time as an underfunctioner. I found myself challenged to acknowledge my natural tendency (overfunctioning) and work for a while (in my opinion) underfunctioning until the system acclimated to a middle ground for all of us.

### *Biblical Stewardship*

We've already looked at how wise stewardship means thinking well about the power we hold, the sacrifice and love required, and the experience of transformation/culture-shaping. Scripture speaks to stewardship in some engaging ways, so it's to the biblical narrative we now turn.

Genesis 1 and 2 describe part of the role that image-bearers take in the world. At the crescendo of creation, Adam and Eve were formed out of the dust of the earth in the image of God himself (Genesis 1:27). This image means that humans are made for connection to God and reflection of God, all for God's own glory.[2] Out of these two foundations comes the role of steward over creation. The couple's marching orders included instructions to:

> "Be fruitful and multiply! Fill the earth and subdue it! Rule over the fish of the sea and the birds of the air and every creature that moves on the ground." Then God said, "I now give you every seed-bearing plant on the face of the entire earth and every tree that has fruit with seed in it. They will be yours for food. And to all the animals of the earth, and to every bird of the air, and to all the creatures that move on the ground—everything that has living breath in it—I give every green plant for food." It was so. (Genesis 1:28–30)

The description provided in Genesis 2:15 notes that humans are to care for and maintain creation. There's an active involvement in the work of stewardship, both of investment toward care and an understanding of the way things ought to be. To maintain something we need to know the ideal, or at least the standard in order for appropriate good care to be enacted.

Intertwined with their image-bearer identity is the role of oversight of the earth. Stewardship from the beginning has been about making something of this place, cultivating out of what God has already breathed into existence. There's a sense in which God has given over the planet to us (yet, of course, not abdicated his own oversight as we will see next) so that we can use, build, and enjoy what is here. We cannot separate our role as stewards from our identity as image-bearers. The image bearing is the dignity out of which we serve as stewards.

With the practice of attention, the fruitfulness of stewardship can be seen. Paul's letter to the Galatian church offers an example of how a community could benefit from a wise steward:

> [6:1]Brothers and sisters, if a person is discovered in some sin, you who are spiritual restore such a person in a spirit of gentleness. Pay close attention to yourselves, so that you are not tempted too. [2]Carry one another's burdens, and in this way you will fulfill the law of Christ. [3]For if anyone thinks he is something when he is nothing, he deceives himself. [4]Let each one examine his own work. Then he can take pride in himself and not compare himself with someone else. [5]For each one will carry his own load.
>
> [6]Now the one who receives instruction in the word must share all good things with the one who teaches it. [7]Do not be deceived. God will not be made a fool. For a person will reap what he sows, [8]because the person who sows to his own flesh will reap corruption from the flesh, but the one who sows to the Spirit will reap eternal life from the Spirit. [9]So we must not grow weary in doing good, for in due time we will reap, if we do not give up. [10]So then, whenever we have an opportunity, let us do good to all people, and especially to those who belong to the family of faith. (Galatians 6:1–10)

The church in Galatia had complex issues related to both morality and community life, so their leaders required both sensitivity and logistical know-how. Just from this passage we can discern some of the underlying issues present. First, there was corruption in the community, and nobody really knew what to do about it (v. 1). Second, there was a strong sense of individuality coupled with some elements of pride (vv. 2–6), and finally, the community was shortsighted in pursuit of their Christian life (vv. 7–9). They lacked spiritual maturity and interdependence. Paul confronts them about this and pleads with them to better engage in the life into which God has called them.

Paul explains that there is a different way in which they can engage with each other. He invites them to gentleness (v. 1), humility (v. 2), self-reflection and not judging others (v. 4), and goodness (vv. 9–10). Partially what the church at Galatia needs is a wise administrator, postured with gentleness, humility, and goodness. For a corrupt and lost community to move toward better things, gentleness is required for the steward. This community needs a humble servant to draw people into a system of interdependence, teaching them how to faithfully bear each other's burdens. The community needs someone to call them into the long view because change and maturity take time.

One of the most difficult things in the world of administration relates to verse 4—the call to focus on our own work and not judge others. It is all too easy for administrators to be judgy toward others—because others lack the acumen we have, because others lack appreciation for the work of the administrator, because they do the work the "wrong" way, and a thousand reasons more. Paul calls his readers to focus on doing their best with their own lives. When we do that, we can carry our own burdens and we also have capacity to carry the burdens of others as needed, which is our great privilege.

### *Dominion*

In direct contrast to the idea of stewardship is the practice of "dominion," or maintaining control over something or someone, which in this context is not what we hope for. The difference between the two comes down to care versus control. When I seek control, it's my agenda that we pursue and the well-being of others may not enter the picture. When I care for something or someone, there is openness in the relationship, the creation of a new experience or opportunity, and well-being or flourishing is part of the goal. It's impossible to control an ecosystem, but we can care for what we have responsibility for and see what grows.

Good stewardship requires self-giving, expertise, and the well-being of the steward. Poor stewardship, or dominion, is characterized by selfishness, a lack of the right kind of skill needed, and also poorly practicing boundaries. Dominion is more about the exhibition of power than the cultivation of growth. In a world where the temptation of dominion abounds, faithful stewardship of an organizational ecosystem invites appropriate boundaries with responsibilities, as well as freedom.

Joseph, the patriarch in Genesis, was a wonderfully gifted steward who practiced good care in an incredibly powerful manner, which partially came out of the dominion he experienced from his brothers and Egyptian masters. Joseph's story, from upstart young dreamer to seasoned administrator of Egypt, is one of developing key competencies that enabled him to save his family, as well as Egypt, in a time of crisis. While Joseph was young, a mixture of naïveté and positivity contributed to his decision to share the dreams he had been having with his family. Maybe he did not realize the depth of animosity his brothers had toward him, or perhaps he simply hoped they wouldn't go as far as they did when they attempted to murder him in jealousy. Regardless, his lack of care in those relationships probably partially contributed to his being sold into slavery. His refining occurred in formidable contexts: a dysfunctional household and prison. Joseph's stewardship was forged in response to those whose manner of being was dominion.

The greatest demonstration of Joseph's reaction to dominion is interwoven with his trust in God. We see this in how he treats his brothers when he holds the second-greatest position of power in Egypt: "Do not be distressed and do not be angry with yourselves for selling me here, because it was to save lives that God sent me ahead of you" (Genesis 45:5 NIV). Joseph's courage is seen throughout his life, as he endured much hardship—from his first night in the cistern, to the unfamiliarity of being in an Egyptian's house, to negotiating life in jail, to organizing economic relief for the world. Joseph kept on with the tasks before him. His administrative acumen is impressive, as he figured out how to faithfully steward all these different kinds of spaces—a wealthy home, a prison, and an empire. He contextualized his stewardship with agility. The test of Joseph's transformed character came when his brothers arrived in Egypt to ask for food during the worldwide famine. From not lashing out in anger, to developing a shrewd plan to test if their hearts had changed, to calming their anxiety once his identity was revealed, Joseph attended to his own emotional state while kindly looking out for that of others. He did not pursue dominion over those who sought his death and caused him great harm—he pursued faithfulness instead.

At the end of his life, Jacob blessed his sons, and, as he spoke to Joseph, evidence of Joseph's transformation into a wise steward was present in that message:

> "Joseph is a fruitful bough,
> a fruitful bough near a spring
> whose branches climb over the wall.
> The archers will attack him,
> they will shoot at him and oppose him.
> But his bow will remain steady,
> and his hands will be skillful;
> because of the hands of the Powerful One of Jacob,
> because of the Shepherd, the Rock of Israel."
>
> (Genesis 49:22–24)

Joseph was effective, growing and bearing fruit in spite of profound challenges. Jacob's assessment of how that happened speaks to the foundation: we steward in this manner because of our relationship with God. Jacob saw what is the key for all who would strive to faithfully administrate in this manner: we can journey through—whatever may come—because of the greatness of the Shepherd who cares for us and provides for us, and because of the security of our Rock, our strong foundation. Thanks be to God!

### *Tool Kit: Forgiveness*

Forgiveness may be the most important tool of all—both asking for it and offering it. If we have not learned how to forgive, we are prone to bitterness and anger, and we carry a burden we are not meant to carry.

Sometimes forgiveness is not pursued because it's hard work. In it we let go of our anger, which often feels like a safer place to dwell. Anger is familiar, while freedom carries the unknown. Among the hurts that administrators suffer are being looked down upon, being taken advantage of, being overlooked and undervalued, and being ignored, not listened to, or scorned for our contributions. Administrators also have tendencies that may require us to ask for the forgiveness of others—sometimes we are judgmental, shortsighted, too task-focused that we neglect to love others, and more!

L. Gregory Jones, a theologian and administrator, invites us to consider what is involved in the practice of forgiving someone.[3] It is noteworthy that he uses the term "practice"—a practice is embodiment and repetition designed to develop a skill or a type of knowledge in us. It's about learning, so that we do a certain thing in a certain way. Coaches have their players rehearse skills, plays, and scenarios so when they get into the game, they can just do it. Musicians practice so their bodies just know which finger to use for which note. Think about the Christian life and some of the practices we employ—we read Scripture often and deeply so the truth of who God is and who we are settles into our minds and hearts so we live in the world in a certain way. Forgiveness as a practice means we learn forgiveness step by step and then grow to become a certain kind of person in the world. It may not be easy, but the goal is that being a forgiving person is who we are.

Forgiving at its essence is not holding someone's sins up as a barrier between us. Jones describes three aspects of this. First, we give up certain claims against each other, such as saying "she is a liar" or "he is a cheater."[4] Then, we give the truth when we assess our relationship. We may need to note that it's broken in certain ways and that we have contributed to the brokenness. We give gifts of ourselves in engaging with the person in a new way. We ask, how will I, an image-bearer of God, treat the person who is also an image-bearer and hurt me? This requires vulnerability and may cause me pain.[5]

Jones describes a "dance of forgiveness," which includes steps that are performed toward the expression of forgiveness. It's a rhythm we enter into.

- We become willing to speak truthfully and patiently about the conflicts that have arisen.
- We acknowledge both the existence of anger and bitterness and a desire to overcome them.
- We summon up a concern for the well-being of the other as a child of God.
- We recognize our own complicity in conflict, remember that we have been forgiven in the past, and take the step of repentance.
- We make a commitment to struggle to change whatever causes and continues to perpetuate our conflicts.
- We confess our yearning for the possibility of reconciliation.[6]

Do we really take it seriously when the Lord's Prayer says, "Forgive us our debts as we forgive our debtors"? What does that really mean? Or, in Matthew 6:14: "For if you forgive other people when they sin against you, your heavenly Father will also forgive you" (NIV)? Is forgiveness an obligation? Absolutely. Does it also lead to our good, delight, and flourishing? Absolutely.

Jones quotes Christian Duquoc: "Forgiveness is an invitation to the imagination."[7] Kevin Vanhoozer describes imagination as "the means for seeing what is there (e.g. the meaning of the whole) that the senses alone are unable to state. The imagination is our port of entry into other modes of experience, into other modes of seeing and thinking, and as such is the unique and indispensable condition of participating in the communicative action of others."[8] This kind of intentional being in the world, directed toward participation with others, is the type of thing we are meant for as Christians. Imagination also helps us develop empathy. For example, if someone responds curtly to your email, you can either think "he's a jerk, so he does obnoxious things," or you can think "he is probably rushing to the deathbed of his beloved grandmother" (or something like that).

While imagination can help us to *be* the right kind of person, it can also help us to *see* rightly. Part of our work is to help paint a hope-filled vision of identity, community, and work—imagining a gospel-shaped life. Vanhoozer calls us toward "eschatological imagination," which is "a faith-based seeing that perceives what is *not yet* complete—our salvation—as *already* finished because of our union with Christ. It is a matter of seeing what is present-partial as future-perfect."[9] An eschatological imagination is one that remembers that any hurts or harms done to us are possible to be forgiven because of what Jesus has done. An eschatological imagination is also one that remembers that any hurts or harms I perform are able to be forgiven because Jesus died for my sins. The forgiveness we experience now we will apprehend wholly one day. In this world we live with one foot in the present reality and one foot in the eschatological reality, moving ever toward that side of things, keeping the long view in sight. We cannot do this without imagination.

Imagination is a meaningful and helpful thing, perhaps even necessary for excellent kingdom work because it calls us to recognize that which is greater than we are. It's not our own determination that gets us out of the pit where we are holding on to hurts and harms. Jesus pulls us out. Recognizing the greatness of God allows us to imagine the immense forgiveness we have been offered through Christ. It calls us to humility and dependence, and directs us to him who is our joy. Forgiveness is much easier when we have heaven in mind.

### *Questions for Reflection*

1. In your administrative role, how do you most often find yourself providing safety and provision as a steward?
2. Do you have a tendency toward overfunctioning or underfunctioning? How does that have an effect on your community or colleagues?
3. What other aspects of the biblical narrative have been helpful to you in understanding administration as stewardship?
4. Are there areas in which you tend toward dominion rather than stewardship? What kind of mind-set could you shift to adapt that?
5. What kinds of people or situations do you find yourself needing to forgive, or needing forgiveness for? What would improving your skills in the dance of forgiveness look like?

# 8

# Figuring Out Fruit

Fruitfulness arrives in a variety of guises in our organizational ecosystems; it is an outward and visual expression of the kingdom breaking into those spaces. Fruitfulness is what overflows from God's work in the world. While the appearance of fruit is not inevitable in our organizations, we have the opportunity to prepare the setting in hope of its arrival. In my experience, I have found that three key competencies related to cultivating space toward fruitfulness in this context are communication, financial management, and assessment. Preparing a helpful perspective on each of these areas leads to the likelihood of the production of fruit. While we fully wait on the Lord to bear it, trusting in his provision and care, wise practice in each of these areas is part of our calling to be responsible gardeners in the ecosystem.

One of the most fascinating explorations of fruitfulness thwarted and fruitfulness exhibited is in Numbers 22 and the story of Balaam's donkey. King Balak (of Moab) is trying to figure out what to do with the Israelites who have been encroaching on his territory. He's not keen on them. He summons the prophet Balaam, who is not sure he wants to come and help this king out. God eventually tells Balaam to go with Balak's men, but the Lord emphasizes that Balaam can only do what God tells him to do (Numbers 22:1–20). So, one day Balaam gets on his donkey to go with the Moabites, and we find out God is angry with his behavior. Suddenly, the angel of the Lord blocks Balaam's path, but Balaam has no clue this is happening. The third time the angel blocks the donkey's path, God opens the donkey's mouth: "What have I done to you that you have beaten me these three times?" (22:28). The donkey asks for trust and humility. It's at this moment that God opens Balaam's eyes to see what the donkey has seen all along. Balaam's response is what we would hope for—he bows to the Lord. What happens next in this exchange is really interesting—the angel of the Lord calls Balaam's path "reckless." This is not in reference to his literal path, but Balaam's posture is reckless because of how many times Yahweh has to warn Balaam to only follow him. Balaam is told both in a dream and by an angel of the Lord that he *must* do only what Yahweh tells him to. We find in verse 39 that Balaam can at least repeat the message that God has given him—it seems as though he has got it by this time.

The next episode in this saga is an ordeal in Numbers 23–24 where Balak pressures Balaam to curse the Israelites, but Balaam ends up giving seven messages to the contrary before Balak gives up and walks away. Seven is a lot of times to repeat yourself—it would have been so difficult to keep on task without Balaam's prior experience with the donkey, ensuring that Balaam was committed to doing things Yahweh's way.

Especially in thinking about fruitfulness, it is so important we pay attention when the way forward is blocked. Sometimes those commonsense messages come from voices we would never expect. Humility and trust are necessary for fruitfulness—if we lack them, the Lord will help us grow in that direction. We may need eyes to see what we are missing. Even as we long to see fruitfulness, we must be committed to only doing what Yahweh tells us to. Sometimes the means to fruitfulness is very different from what we might expect. The Lord is present and gracious still. He did not leave Balaam, and God even gave him a very powerful ministry after his hard-heartedness.

Let's explore the postures and practices that will contribute to the conditions of an environment where fruitfulness is likely to occur.

### *Collaborative Communication*

"Collaborative communication" is a term used to describe what happens when more than one person works toward a goal or on a project—when information must be exchanged and often negotiation must occur. The challenge to such arrangements is that not everyone communicates in the same way, let alone has the same assumptions about what helpful communication looks like. Collaborative communication requires adaptability and creativity, as well as a posture of humility and care.

One important thing to consider is how the idea of collaborative communication is nuanced in different cultures. For example, in a "high-culture" context, to get to a collaborative conversation, the path will not be direct, whereas "low-culture" contexts are highly individualistic and personal space and privacy are valued, along with direct verbal communication. In high-culture contexts, communication relies heavily on the environment and the group's values and is often indirect, leaning on interpersonal relationships. When I worked in a high-culture context, if a colleague talked to me about congregational involvement in small groups, for example, that meant congregational involvement in small groups was an issue to which I should pay attention. Moving to a low-culture context, I eventually realized that similar conversations were just that—interesting conversations—and if my supervisor wanted me to engage that problem, he would tell me. Our own preference may be complicated since communication has been modeled for us in a certain way. There may also be communication expectations in our contexts, so we may have to adapt to unfamiliar communication styles in order to better serve those around us. Communication in a diverse team requires a high level of sensitivity and the choice to communicate in a way that may not be natural to me for the sake of the mission. Ecosystems survive best when communication within the group of organisms occurs regularly.

Two anchors of collaborative communication are cohesive narratives and integrative meaning making.

*Cohesive narratives.* How did the organizations in which you were a part make sense of what happened through the pandemic? During the spring of 2020, as the world was developing our understanding of what the coronavirus was going to mean to us, a great leadership challenge and opportunity arose. We grappled with fear of the unknown and death, morphing to the never-ending frustration of limitations, and the anxiety of the "new normal." Thrown in there was navigating different perspectives on what was going on, as well as politicization and polarization. Maybe the organization was already on perilous ground prior to the pandemic. At the organization where I worked, the image our president used was that we were a caravan facing both a drought and a windstorm. Survival depended on finding new resources while preserving the resources we already had, and it meant circling up and supporting each other in the storm. That became our guiding cohesive narrative for that season. It was a wonderful help to refer to that story to shepherd us through uncertainty. That creative image helped us tell our story in an accessible way that both gave meaning to our experience and provided hope for the future.[1] That image propped the community up because it meant that our collective experience had coherency and language—it was understandable why we were weary and depleted.

*Integrative meaning making.* Collaborative communication ought to lead to integrative meaning making, the experience of putting together a coherent explanation of all we are and all we do in our organizational ecosystem. We cannot integrate without listening to and learning from others. Additionally, whatever meaning we come up with must be communicated holistically so everyone understands what is going on and connects it to their experience. When I first started working in higher education administration, I noticed that my boss and his boss regularly ended the day with fun, raucous laughter, full of teasing and hilarity. I'd sometimes go over to their offices and join in, finding it to be a great stress relief concluding an intense day. As I got to know each of these men better, I realized that ending the day like this was intentional because, as the vice president would say, "If you don't laugh, you'll cry." This was his way of bringing his team together, finding meaning through our shared challenges, and shepherding us into a new perspective. Collaborative communication means listening empathetically to stakeholders and drawing everyone into the cohesive narrative, reminding them again and again of why we are doing what we are doing. When that is done collaboratively, we don't alienate others but create a sense of unity. Everyone knows the story in which we find ourselves.

To get to the point where communication is a catalyst in the work, clarity around several matters related to collaboration needs to be pursued.

- Each person ought to be clear on the goals of communication and the priorities therein—is the communication meant to build trust, complete tasks, avoid awkwardness, create something innovative, or something else?
- What are the boundaries in place? This could be personal comfort zones, time or spatial boundaries of when and how communication is expected, formats for communication, etc. Not everyone envisions collaboration in the same way. For instance, if one party assumes that hallway conversations mean approval and another party assumes casual chats are for awareness only, trouble comes when trying to move forward with people who did not think they were giving support, just absorbing information.
- Is everyone aware that collaboration is expected? Depending on high- or low-culture context, not everyone recognizes expectations around collaboration. Thus, everyone may not be aware of the challenges of collaborative communication relevant to the team.
- Building and rebuilding trust again and again must happen for collaborative conversation to get somewhere. When we enter into a conversation with skepticism and baggage, it's much more challenging to move forward because of all the extra "stuff" in the way.
- When conflict arises, are parties equipped with both the emotional intelligence and skills needed to navigate those issues? Is the team prepared to expect that persistence and adaptation are vital?
- How are meetings used? Are they for status updates, brainstorming, decision making, or something else? Is everyone on the team satisfied with how meeting time is being used?

- Are the tools for communication (technology, schedule, and time) sufficient for the goals of the organization? If the tools are insufficient, precious time and energy will be wasted.

If people find themselves contributing to agendas and conversations, that's a sign that collaboration is welcome. Whether or not the collaboration is helpful is another question. Will others be willing to challenge when reasoning is laid out? For example, if I think that X is the right direction, and when I explain how I got to that point, will others tell me if that seems reasonable or will they silently disagree? Finally, genuine collaboration requires that others are as invested as I am, which can be demonstrated by sharing the load or by follow-through taking place.

### *Finances*

Some of the most interesting conversation partners in an organization work in finance and accounting. They have a unique and bird's-eye perspective to help us see overall themes and trends we might miss. In an ecosystem, dealing with money must include reflections on how finances will impact how we interact and fulfill our mission. The process of building and managing a budget is not performed in a vacuum or on a spreadsheet alone, but it's done in conversation and with stakeholders. In addition to looking at numbers, we need to manage other people's expectations and develop a culture of assessment so we are knowledgeable about how money and mission interact. This requires collaborative communication. But first, here are some basic foundational guidelines on how to build and manage a budget.

*Building a budget.* The essence of building a budget includes starting with the necessary expenses, adding them all up, and organizing them over time. That's the budget. Wisdom, however, accounts for a variety of factors, including prioritizing spending for the mission, understanding fixed costs and flexibility, looking at goals, regularly monitoring spending, and adjusting as needed. There are no shortcuts to understanding a budget—it takes time, careful attention to both the big picture and the details, asking the right questions, and evaluation year to year and often month to month. Building a budget sometimes means asking questions, performing tasks and reading spreadsheets that are uncomfortable for us. Perhaps the most difficult aspect of the task is our limited knowledge—if only we could confidently forecast the future and then build the budget off of that! When organizational health or survival is at stake, it can be difficult to build a budget in faith, yet that is often what is required. Perhaps more than most administrative tasks, making a budget requires deep attentiveness to God's voice and sensitivity to his nudging, which can be easily lost in the complex process and details. Yet, because our plans depend on an unseen future, our need for guidance is extraordinarily evident.

*Managing a budget.* The basic principles of a budget for an organization or a department are similar to those of a personal or family budget: tracking what comes in and what goes out. The challenges come in the particulars: At what intervals is the money coming in, and how regular is the income? What assurance is there that the same amount of money will come in at the interval needed? Does the money going out coincide with the money coming in, or is there a deficit at some point of the year? Success in managing a budget lies in tracking the money. A financial dashboard (a brief report containing key indicators of health) is a great tool—categories can be tracked year to year so decision makers can tell when there is growth or decline. Knowledge and familiarity of the budget depend on accurate, clear, and communicable data. If the numbers are in the wrong places, if the decision makers cannot track what the report is trying to say, or if they don't get the report, leading wisely is impossible.

Numbers always tell a story, and part of the integrity needed in managing budgets is telling the story truthfully, accurately, and helpfully. Those who manage budgets in an organization need collaborative communication skills just as much, or possibly more than, they need accounting skills. Because organizations change over time, it can feel as though the narrative changes as well—as it should. But those of us who hear the narrative from budget managers are tempted to question the past and wonder about the integrity of the storyteller. Each person involved in understanding the budget has a responsibility to understand the story, evaluate the data, and ensure that healthy resource management is being pursued, all the while paying attention to the temptations present for each task. Are we listening empathetically? Are we evaluating objectively? Are we stewarding resources responsibly and biblically?

In his book *The Business of the Church*, John W. Wimberly Jr. describes churches as systems, and he shares implications of this reality.[2] A system such as a church contains a number of smaller systems—children, youth, outreach, etc.—and if we navigate the smaller systems well, the larger one works better. We are interrelated and interdependent both in the body of Christ in the spiritual sense and in the systems-thinking sense! We have to think about parts in relation to their system—siloed approaches are trouble. Good financial management of an organization, whether as a whole or in a department, will lead to fewer instances of fraud or theft. We have the opportunity to reduce the temptation of misuse or mismanagement of resources when we have a thoughtful system. Financial data is subject to multiple interpretations just like most other kinds of data. If we are wise in how we read, asking good questions, that will serve our understanding and our organizations well.

Key differences exist between organizational budgets and personal budgets. Organizational budgets are more complex and usually require software to track things because of the different rhythms of income and expenses. Payroll must be accounted for—personnel costs are usually the most significant expenses in an organization. "Deferred maintenance" is when money is set aside in case repairs for assets are needed, like installing a new roof even though the current roof is fine. For some organizations, funding deferred maintenance is a requirement. Fund-raising is often a part of organizational finances. A key part of fund-raising is endowment—a legal structure for managing and, in many cases, indefinitely perpetuating a pool of investments, real estate, etc., for a specific purpose according to the intent of founders and donors. Endowments help with stability for organizations when they work as intended. Most institutional budgets will require both an income statement (a record of income and expenses) and a balance sheet (assets and liabilities). A cash flow report shows how much cash is on hand. We have to know our deficits and surpluses to be able to build a responsible budget. The goal is financial stability—knowing what's coming in and what's going out, with limited surprises. A wonderful test of the true measure of our hearts is what happens when surprises come. Do good surprises lead us immediately to worship? Are we quick to share about a windfall of resources even when it's possible others will stake a claim on them? Do difficult surprises lead us to despair, anger, or hurt? Are we sharing difficult news appropriately, especially if we sense shame or judgmentalism?

It usually takes several cycles (often annual ones) to really get a handle on what is going on with the finances of an organization. Just because it takes a while to understand the financial picture does not mean there is a problem; it just means a plethora of factors are involved, and it takes time and attention to gain appropriate familiarity. Those of us not involved in the finances can help those who directly manage the finances, for whom accuracy is key. Submitting reimbursements in a timely manner is really important. Accurately accounting for how money comes in and goes out is also important. Do not round numbers. Also, ignoring the budget is tantamount to a straight-up slap in the face to many accountants! For both budget managers and budget spenders, humility is key as we try to care well for each other.

Scripture speaks often about money, and the principles it conveys work for organizations as well as individuals. We are told to not bury our resources in the sand but to use them. Consider risks wisely, but risks can get us to great places (Matthew 25:24–30). God blesses those who give cheerfully—that means we do what we can to facilitate the cheerfulness of givers, and the organization itself should cheerfully give (2 Corinthians 9:7). When organizations find beauty, joy, and appreciation for the widow's mite, that honors God (Luke 21:1–4). Loving money is the root of all kinds of evil (1 Timothy 6:10), and money never satisfies (Ecclesiastes 5:10).

The formation that happens in the world of finance often shows up in the state of one's heart toward others. I had a job years ago that required me to record the financial gifts of others. It was a weekly struggle to not judge givers based on what I saw come in. Sometimes it was so evident when someone gave with joy, and sometimes it was clear when someone gave because they sought influence and attention. When someone gave with generosity, it was like a wonderful secret that I got to keep. Those who work in finance often get to see up close God's abundant provision—sometimes at the eleventh hour or in ways we least expect. Reading a balance sheet and remembering the stories behind the numbers is an opportunity for a unique way to worship.

One's integrity is of primary importance when working with finances. So much of our posture and decisions is decided in secret. Character is how we react even before our brain fully processes the situation. This is about a commitment to transparency and welcoming scrutiny because it serves us and our organizations well. The posture of not being judgmental is so important, even as we pursue joy in dire situations. Generosity of spirit and practice is key for anyone who has a budget (that's all of us!).

### *Developing a Culture of Assessment*

One of the best ways to demonstrate integrity is by developing a culture of assessment. Assessment is the way we measure our people, policies, and programs in the world of administration. Having a *culture* of assessment means we do this regularly so that it's the air that we breathe in our organizations and our decisions are data-informed. Pursuing a culture of assessment in our organizations is about demonstrating we do what we say we do, and it provides us with a process for continual improvement. Ignoring the practice of assessment means that we subject ourselves to mere whims and opinions, whether from people inside the organization or outside. However, clearly demonstrating that we accomplish our mission means we care about our integrity as an organization. Paying attention to our integrity in this way is part of our witness to the world. When suspicion of leaders and organizations is a growing part of our culture, when trust wanes, showing that we are who we purport to be, telling the truth about what we do, means we are caring well for our organizations, and for those who would engage with us.

The challenge present in assessment work is that we value what we count; that means we have to make sure we are "counting" the most important things. In churches, we usually look to attendance, buildings, and cash as our markers of success. If assessment isn't in its right place, we tend to develop both fear and idols along the way. We wonder if we are "good enough," or we begin to think we may not really need the Lord. Our identity may be affected by how we understand our assessment. King David faced a harsh punishment resulting from his choice to take a census (1 Chronicles 21).

There are two main ways to do assessments: quantitatively and qualitatively. Quantitative assessment looks at the numbers. For example: How many people come to an event? What's our bottom line? How satisfied is someone on a likert scale with our program? (A likert scale asks people to assign numbers to their attitude or opinion, usually on a five- or seven-point spread.) Quantitative assessments are often done with surveys and spreadsheets, or other ways of counting what is measured.

Qualitative assessment looks at how someone experienced something. It's about understanding how people make meaning out of experiences. It's narrow in scope and is not meant to make generalizations. For example, if I say, "Tom described his experience of the retreat as life-giving," that does not mean everyone did—it means that Tom did. When we are writing qualitative reports and reading them, we need to interpret with a certain discerning lens. Interviews and observations are generally how we get to this kind of data.

Both qualitative and quantitative data have value in different ways since they answer different questions. It's important to collect and not ignore the data that puts us in a less than positive light. A healthy culture of assessment should be part of the rhythm of the organization, and the data should be communicated to all stakeholders for the sake of transparency and integrity. Ideally, the data is easily accessible and referred to often by decision makers.

In Matthew 14 John the Baptist has died, and Jesus attempts to take time to rest and grieve. Instead, the crowds follow him, and their needs are myriad. Jesus heals the people and feeds them, and then he sends his disciples and the people away. After spending time by himself, Jesus then goes to meet the disciples. There's so much assessment that happens in this chapter! After his self-assessment, Jesus goes to pray. When he comes back, he assesses the crowds—they need healing and food. After that, he assesses the disciples and gets them away from the crowds so they can rest. We find that Peter wants an assessment of Jesus—if it *is* Jesus on the water, he'd like an invitation to join Jesus out there. Of course, when Jesus affirms that it is him, Peter gets out of the boat, assesses the situation, and loses his trust. Jesus, thankfully, assesses that Peter is drowning and has little faith. After the rescue, Peter gives the final assessment in this chapter, directed toward Jesus. He confidently says, "Truly you are the Son of God" (Matthew 14:33). In this chapter we see the heart of assessment: it is the demonstration that someone (or some organization) is who they say they are and does what they say they can do. Jesus is truly the epitome of that.

Because assessment is essentially about integrity, we need to make sure we are honestly and helpfully assessing ourselves. When do we need to go off by ourselves? We need to be willing to meet the needs around us, even when it may not be convenient. Perhaps there were other ways Jesus would have chosen to grieve. Our context can give us clues about our self-assessment—Peter sunk in the sea because he had little faith. What does our context clue us into about ourselves? Most importantly, when we're thinking about Jesus, our assessment of him can and ought to turn into worship. It is an act of faith because we only see and know in part, but one day that will be greatly expanded. What a day that will be!

### *Tool Kit: Leading Meetings*

Since one of the primary contexts for facilitating collaborative communication, finances, and assessment is meetings, below is a basic checklist for planning meetings.

1. Know the purpose of the meeting. Why do you need these people in a particular space at the same time? This is about honoring the time and energy of participants—caring well for them in the process you invite them into.
2. Tell them about the purpose of the meeting. Make sure it's clear why you are gathering *this* group of people. Communication of that could happen in a variety of means—hallway conversations, emails, calendar invites, etc.—but make sure they are as clear as you are about why you are requesting their time and energy. If possible, connect this meeting's purpose to your organization's or department's mission.
3. Prepare an agenda. Know what topics will be discussed and how much time you will allot for them. Communicate the agenda to your attendees. Be clear in the agenda about your plans for each topic: you are communicating info, asking for feedback, taking a vote as part of a collective decision, etc. The kindness of a clear agenda is demonstrated when participants come with meaningful contributions, which is possible because the organizer has given them the impetus to prepare well.
4. Account for the logistics. When and where will you be meeting? What can you do to prepare the space so your purpose is most effectively accomplished? Will you provide a meal or water, pens, and notebooks? Is the temperature and lighting right? Is it a safe space? Small details communicate care and facilitate both connection and contributions.

5. Have necessary conversations ahead of time so any barriers to your purpose are addressed beforehand. Can you find allies who will positively contribute to the conversation? What questions can you answer for naysayers so they have time to process ahead of time? When a meeting organizer is convinced that each participant has gifts to bring to the meeting, the premeeting conversations serve to build healthy anticipation and prepare the way for those gifts to be presented.
6. Decide whether the meeting will follow Robert's Rules of Order. Robert's Rules is an agreed-upon way to run meetings and follow parliamentary procedure to ensure clarity and fairness in decision making. If your group will be using it, be prepared with a review of procedure. While a full rule book is published and updated regularly, Wikipedia has a helpful summary and simplified versions are available online. Even if Robert's Rules is not used for your meeting, clarity on how decisions will be made is vital (whether unanimity, supermajority, or simple majority is necessary, for example), and how much space will be given to the minority opinion to express their views must also be communicated. Clarity in meeting protocol is about stewarding power well.
7. Make sure participants are clear on what they are being asked to do as follow-up of the meeting. Provide the minutes/notes on what happened at the meeting to ensure that everyone knows where you are going next. This is about integrity—does your group make decisions in word only, or is follow-through present so that what is decided is enacted?

A common sentiment in organizations is that meetings are a waste of time and should be eliminated so the real work can get done. That often is true. However, meetings can also be time-savers and provide an energetic boon. They metaphorically allow us to take the hands of the people in the room and ask, "Will you go with me?" as we try to live into our organization's mission in our particular ecosystem.

## *Questions for Reflection*

1. What have you observed about your organization's cohesive narratives and integrative meaning making? Are they effective? Could anything be adjusted so that these have a more prominent role in communications?
2. There are many potential pitfalls and challenges related to finances. Math mistakes can be pretty easily fixed, but relationships are more difficult to repair. In the context of working with a team of people on a budget, what do people tend to get annoyed about? What do you tend to get annoyed by?
3. How are you doing at managing the various budgets in your responsibility? Are they consistent with your mission and goals? Does anything need to be adjusted?
4. Spend some time in reflection, assessing yourself and your integrity. Are there any areas of your life where what you say and do are not consistent? Are there areas of your spiritual life in which you need to take stock and do an evaluation?
5. Whether you plan meetings or attend them (most likely, both!), what are your strengths, and what are your unhelpful tendencies? How can you adjust to better serve the group in the meeting setting?

# 9

# How Do We Pray?

How do we pray as administrators?

Some days are so difficult, the only thing to do is pray.

Some situations, seasons, and jobs are so challenging that we find ourselves being transformed into one for whom communion with God is not only our means of coping but also our joy. The complexity of our context compels us to come in humility to our heavenly Father, who delights in giving us good gifts when we ask. In this chapter, we are going to reflect on becoming the kind of person for whom prayer is not only our reflex in desperation but also the sustaining rhythm of our whole lives. I write as someone who is not an expert in prayer, but rather a regular practitioner and evangelist for the strengthening refuge of God through prayer.

Psalm 91 has long been my go-to during those challenging times:

> 1As for you, the one who lives in the shelter of
>     the Most High,
> and resides in the protective shadow of
>     the Sovereign One—
> 2I say this about the LORD, my shelter and my stronghold,
> my God in whom I trust—
> 3he will certainly rescue you from the snare of the hunter
> and from the destructive plague.
> 4He will shelter you with his wings;
> you will find safety under his wings.
> His faithfulness is like a shield or a protective wall.

[5]You need not fear the terrors of the night,
the arrow that flies by day,
[6]the plague that stalks in the darkness,
or the disease that ravages at noon.
[7]Though a thousand may fall beside you,
and a multitude on your right side,
it will not reach you.
[8]Certainly you will see it with your very own eyes—
you will see the wicked paid back.
[9]For you have taken refuge in the Lord,
my shelter, the Most High.
[10]No harm will overtake you;
no illness will come near your home.
[11]For he will order his angels
to protect you in all you do.
[12]They will lift you up in their hands,
so you will not slip and fall on a stone.
[13]You will subdue a lion and a snake;
you will trample underfoot a young lion and a serpent.
[14]The Lord says,
"Because he is devoted to me, I will deliver him;
I will protect him because he is loyal to me.
[15]When he calls out to me, I will answer him.
I will be with him when he is in trouble;
I will rescue him and bring him honor.
[16]I will satisfy him with long life,
and will let him see my salvation." (Psalm 91)

This psalm is an invitation to make our home in the haven that is Yahweh. It's a testimony of what God does for his people—he provides them with exactly the help they need when they need it. The confidence of the psalmist in verse 5 is powerful—there is no doubt that God will save, no matter the enemy, no matter the attack. The reason for his confidence is the communion he has with the Lord.

> For you have taken refuge in the LORD,
> my shelter, the Most High. (v. 9)

God provides for us.

The foundation of an effective prayer life as an administrator, a steward of an organizational ecosystem, is a core conviction that the Lord will provide all we need. This chapter reflects on postures and practices that direct us toward that end.

### *Be Still*

In our world of emails, messages, to-do lists, meetings, projects, and deadlines, we risk being carried along by the pressures of the work rather than by the presence of God, if we do not develop the capacity to be still (Psalm 46:10). Being still means stopping intentionally and quieting our hands so our minds and our hearts can be quiet as well. In that quietness we find the person who is our true desire. There's no shortcut to stillness, no substitute possible. The only thing to do is stop, take some sort of step away mentally or physically, and remember who God is. In the stillness we also gain perspective on who we are. Prayer happens without stillness, of course. Prayer also happens differently in the stillness, and the difference is in our awareness of our attachment to God.

Jim Wilder and Michel Hendricks describe the role of attachment to God as part of how our brains are wired to engage in spiritual formation.[1] They observe our tendency to live in our left brains, where conscious thought, speech, strategy, problem solving, logic, and stories take the primary role, over our right brains, where individual identity, group identity, emotional attunement to others, assessment of surroundings, and relational attachment dwell.[2] They note that spiritual growth is governed by the right side of the brain, which requires relationality and attachment.[3] Retraining our brains for relationality and attachment means that we start with stillness, focusing on the joy of relationship and the connectedness we have with God.

There are, of course, very helpful practical things that create space for stillness: entering into a different physical space, setting alarms to make sure we prioritize it, and understanding what it takes for our minds to get to a place of stillness. It all begins with a decision that stillness is important enough to take precedence over work, and to sometimes find places for it within the work.

When I am not still, I find that there's a lie that creeps in that causes me to run from it. The lie is that if I walk away from the work, God won't be able to accomplish his purposes. The truth is that I can trust God enough to stop. This is often why we don't prioritize Sabbath. Sabbath includes engagement with others and ensures that we are living fully into our humanity as image-bearers, but it is also a practice of faith that things will not fall apart if we stop working for a period of time.

Sometimes in God's goodness, he creates space for us to be still. It happens in a variety of ways—sometimes illness, sometimes canceled meetings, sometimes transportation challenges, sometimes even more severe situations. A student told me about a season where all of those things converged in life at the same time, with the addition of a lost job, no opportunity to take classes, and even no phone. In that stillness her loving heavenly Father garnered her attention and met her in that desperation. She told me she previously never understood why stillness was necessary because it was not common in her cultural background, but once God got her attention, she was beginning to realize how full that stillness really was. Stillness gives us an opportunity to sense the presence of God, to recognize his nearness. Exodus 14:14 reminds us, "The Lord will fight for you, and you can be still."

### *Be Listening*

Stillness means that we are ready to pay attention, to listen. It's a subtle shift in energy—whereas in silence we focus on ceasing, in a posture of listening we offer our attention somewhere. As we sense the presence of God, we move our hearts and ears so we are ready to hear from God. For me, I have a visual cue that reminds me to ask God each morning that I would be quick to listen to his Spirit: as soon as I approach the steps to the door to my building, I ask God for ears to hear him that day. I also have a practice of taking a quick lunchtime walk to give my brain time and space to mull over the complexities of the morning, listening for God's nudges (some days necessitate a late afternoon ramble as well!).

Listening well requires courage. I led a committee that was tasked with making a difficult decision, and our collective discernment required significant wrestling. One member of the committee regularly noticed when we were not all on the same page, and several times invited us to take an extra week to reflect and pray before moving on. His gift of seeing where each of us was in our discernment process and inviting us to pause because we were not ready for the next phase was invaluable. It was a bold request because he called us to vulnerability, humility, and dependence on God and each other.

Giving our attention to God is easily overlooked in the practice of prayer. We are usually eager to give him our needs (and he is eager to receive them!), but often the attentiveness to God in prayer is glossed over in favor of unburdening ourselves. Inherent in the role of steward is the capacity to listen, to recognize the voice of our Creator and Lord, who will direct us in the ways that we should go.

The assumption in the direction "be listening" is that God will speak and we are able to hear him. John 1 is an incredible confirmation of the nearness of God, as well as his propensity to be listened to. John begins all the way back: "*In the beginning* was the Word . . ." From the start, God has described himself to us as ready to communicate with his creation. We find in John 1:14 that God's communicable actions extend even further to the incarnation, becoming enfleshed, demonstrating his willingness to speak if we will listen. "Now the Word became flesh and took up residence among us. We saw his glory—the glory of the one and only, full of grace and truth, who came from the Father." If Jesus was so willing to leave heaven to come near to us, we can be assured that he will speak at the right time and in the right way. We need only to listen.

### *Be Asking*

Listening in a relationship is dialogue, and it is God's expectation that we come to him asking for things. He welcomes requests because they are indicative of our conviction that we are in need, coming to the one who can provide for us.

Perhaps the key in asking with faith is the request for the right thing at the right time. Often we assume we know the right thing for our situation, and we end up disappointed when we look around for it. Sometimes we do understand what the right thing is, but we assume we also know the right timing for the right thing. Getting the thing and the time right is so difficult, so I've taken to just asking the Lord to take care of both of those things. It can be helpful to name what does seem to be the right thing, but to hold that loosely, trusting in the One who has perfect knowledge and perfect power.

When we hold the role of steward, it can be difficult to ask for things because we have assumed a certain level of responsibility. If we ask, we acknowledge our lack, which does not always feel very responsible of us. Asking the Lord for what we need, however, does not necessarily mean we have abdicated our responsibility. My first office job after college was at a custom countertop company where the office manager, George, gave me a wonderful foundation for practices in the workplace—in a quirky guise that, back then, I smiled and rolled my eyes at, but for which I now have so much appreciation. One day I apparently attempted some sort of shortcut on a project. I still remember George in his brightly colored Hawaiian shirt miming in our office how I had tried to give him a monkey when that monkey was firmly attached to me. The monkey is whatever problem an employee tries to transfer to their manager that they really ought to keep and solve themselves. I found out later what book George had read and the principle he was trying to get me to understand.[4] The monkey needs to stay with the appropriate person until it's time to pass it along. To apply the analogy to prayer—the monkey of responsibility for our need may be on our back organizationally speaking, but we are on God's back as we walk around the zoo together. He's got us and all of our monkeys!

### *Be Identified*

Prayers don't come to God as wisps of words floating up from Earth. They emerge from real people. The words flow truthfully when we pray out of our created identities. When we pray as image-bearers and beloved children, we pray out of this precious attachment to our Maker and Father. When I ask for things, standing in the knowledge of how loved I am, that changes everything. Fear fades, insecurity washes away, and I can instead confidently and joyfully speak with God about everything.

Sometimes in our work as administrators we are tempted to pray as organizational loyalists, not as kingdom citizens. We mistakenly assume our organization is central to God's purposes on this earth. What a prideful posture. When I remember that I am instead a member of the kingdom of God—that God's work in the world is directed toward what I cannot see, what will exist into eternity—I can let go of what seems to be important in the little world of my organization. God will always accomplish his purposes, and what I see is only a tiny fraction of that.

### *The Posture of Psalm 91*

The psalmist has taken up permanent residence in God's shelter—that's where he is rooted. He's certain of rescue and safety, regardless of what the enemy may do. There may be horrible people and scenarios swirling around him, but the center truth holds: God is his refuge and strength. The psalmist ends by reminding himself of all that Yahweh will do for him: deliver, protect, answer, be with, rescue, satisfy, and help him to see God's salvation. The entire goal of developing our postures in prayer is to become the kind of person who is in permanent residence in God's shelter. It's a wonderful place to run to, but we are meant to live there, to dwell in the protective shelter of the Sovereign One (Psalm 91:1). Our rootedness there means our trust in God has changed who we are and how we see the world.

### *Tool Kit: Prayer*

Years ago I began a practice of asking experienced administrators how they pray. What follows is a list I've cultivated from their generous conversations with me.

- "Pray lots." This exhortation is a quote directly from my mentor—a woman who faithfully served multiple institutions of Christian higher education over decades. She saw change after change after change, and weathered intense challenges with dignity and grace. She was clear-eyed about what was important in crises. She knew what it meant to be at a dead end and find that God opened a side door unexpectedly. Those unexpected provisions strengthened her faith and caused her to pray more and more. Often when she prays for me, I hear her say, "God, you know . . . ," which I take as a precious affirmation that she speaks with confidence out of her sense of God's presence from her past experiences and her knowledge that I need to be reminded of that presence as well. That exhortation also comes out of knowing that, in the work of administration, God needs to intervene on our behalf, and our job is to ask him to do so.
- Pray boldly. Our God delights in answering our requests. When we pray in faith, with that boldness that signifies our hope, he is so pleased to respond. Sometimes he answers with a dramatic flourish; sometimes it's in the quiet, inviting us to notice the shadow of his hand in the corner. While the exhortation to pray boldly as an administrator comes from my mentor, I have my own experience of seeing God answer a bold prayer in my personal life. When I gradu-

ated from seminary, I spent six years paying off my master's degrees. I had been wondering for many years if a PhD would be in my future, but I did not want to bring debt into a new degree, so waiting those six years caused me to pray that I would not need to take out loans for that next degree. (I had also been praying for a generous benefactor to jump in and pay off those loans, but God's answer to that request was instead a steady job and some side hustles that allowed me to make payments.) I had no sense of how I would manage to pay for a PhD, but nevertheless, it was something I asked God for. Those were difficult years, and it was eventually clear that my time in that position should conclude. Out of the blue, I got a call about a position that opened up and an invitation to apply. The job was at a seminary and included a benefit of two free classes each semester. I graduated with my PhD debt-free, which was amazing, but I am even more grateful for the confidence in the Lord's perfect provision for what I need at the right time and in the right way.

- Pray specifically. This advice was from a CFO, and, while I think that exhortation comes out of an accountant's personality tendencies, it's especially valuable for those of us who are less detail-oriented. Praying specifically is mostly for our benefit. Consequentially we are less likely to miss God's response to us. We are busy, living full and fast-paced lives, but sometimes God's answers stop us in our tracks. How gracious of the Lord to essentially shout at us to "look at this!" when he responds.
- Pray hopefully. In systems prone to scarcity, we need hope. We need the glimmer of expectation that our Savior will come. That's part of shifting from the scarcity mind-set to an abundance mind-set. Praying with hope means we keep the end of the story in mind—not out of pride or avoidance, but as a means of sustenance for the journey. God is on the throne and will always be on that throne—no matter the rebellion that comes, no matter the enemy that arises against him. That is our salvation—he will reign forever and ever.
- Pray for wisdom. The complexity in which we work is overwhelming. The needs never end, and the stewardship required to address

those needs is impossible without wisdom from our Father above. We change, things change, but he does not. His wisdom provides exactly what we need at the right time and in the right way. One practice of prayer that has shaped me immensely has been a daily ritual that invites me to not only pray for wisdom in the abstract, but to ask for help in the practice of wisdom. Over a decade ago I started asking the Lord to help me be "quick to listen, slow to speak, slow to anger" (James 1:19) when I walk into work. It's been a centering practice focusing me on what is most important each day—to provide a nonanxious presence. I've also started tacking on the phrase "and help me listen to your Spirit" as well. The more I work with people and with complex organizations, the more concerned I am about not following in step with what God wants to do. Wisdom comes through the discipline of these kinds of rhythms.

## *Questions for Reflection*

1. How do you pray as an administrator?
2. What are the hindrances to your practices of stillness and silence? What can help you remove the challenges to that?
3. How were you formed as a listener? What contributes to your capacity to listen? What makes it difficult to listen?
4. When you pray, what is your primary identity? With what posture do you enter into God's presence?

# Part 4

## *Imagination*

Imagination begins and thrives in childhood. I have fond memories of childhood imaginative play that my siblings and I engaged in—those golden-hued and carefree hours. Reflecting on those experiences as adults has been fascinating for us. My sister (a therapist) has observed that her role in play has been consistent with how she engages with the world as an adult. We played a lot of "house" and "school," and my sister Lainey always wanted to be in charge of planning the scene. Each of her imaginative episodes had some sort of crazy conflict to work through—anything could happen! In comparison, when I engaged in those imaginative scenarios (often needing to assert my authority as the oldest child to take the boss role away from Lainey), I would have very positive and fun adventures that did not include danger or subterfuge. I think this is why Lainey now works with a high-risk population and my other two siblings and I talk about how we crave low-conflict lives. Understanding this particular experience has allowed her to develop a metaphor for how she sees herself as an imaginative person. She brings all of who she is to her work as a therapist and helps people on the precipice of mental health crises. She invites her clients to imagine how they might resolve their issues and take steps toward a better life. The skill she developed while corralling her siblings toward an imaginative future is serving her well in her career.

Laval St. Germain is an adventurer who, in 2016, *rowed* a boat by himself from Halifax, Canada, to France, about 2,800 miles. Rowing is the only mode of transportation in which you can only see where you have come from and must use your imagination to picture where you are going. St. Germain spent fifty-three days and nights finding the strength, perseverance, and will to survive an incredibly harsh environment only from what he could picture in his mind.[1] On a bike, in a car, or on an airplane, our eyes provide us the picture of where we are going. For St. Germain, his mind held on to what he envisioned while rowing hour after grueling hour. His imagination made his way.

That's how we journey through the Christian life—we may not always see where we are going. It's difficult to visualize the next step in our discipleship, the next thing God will do in a crisis situation, or even what heaven will really be like, but we imagine our way through—imagination helps us make our way. We can, through the guidance of the Holy Spirit, imagine our way toward who God has invited us to become. God calls us to look to him in trust that he will lead us as we make our way. He uses our imagination to do so.

In the next chapter we will look at why we need imagination in our administrative work and how to use it, but first let's explore what imagination is and why it is not typically associated with administrative work.

Gregory Currie and Ian Ravenscroft's book *Recreative Minds* dissects what our brains do in the act of imagination. They say imagination is about "enabling us to project ourselves into another situation and to see, or think about, the world from another perspective. These situations and perspectives are not currently ours, but ones we come to occupy, as we say, in imagination."[2] Imagination moves us to step out from inside our own heads, where we are surrounded by our own experience, and, as Currie and Ravenscroft say, occupy space somewhere else.[3] Part of the fabric of who we are as human beings is imagination. Plus, as we build our plausibility structures (the scaffolding of how we interpret reality so that it makes sense to us), that scaffold is in fact made up of the stuff of imagination. Imagination is mental representations, giving us new perspectives and allowing us to make sense of our world.

We cannot leave imagination only in the hands of philosophers, so let's consider what the artists say about it. Let's also add in a theological component and consider how Christian writers understand imagination.

Luci Shaw is a poet and essayist. She writes, "I cannot turn on the writing art or transcendence like a faucet. My job is to wait and see—literally to *wait* for the Spirit, with the Spirit, and to *see*."[4] She knows that her Creator is the one who gives life to her work as a writer. She is entirely dependent on him to give her sight, or more precisely, *insight* for her words.

Poet, novelist, and essayist Wendell Berry has a similar perspective. In his poem "Sabbath,"[5] he writes,

> The mind that comes to rest is tended
> In ways that it cannot intend:
> Is borne, preserved, and comprehended
> By what it cannot comprehend.
>
> Your Sabbath, Lord, thus keeps us by
> Your will, not ours. And it is fit
>     Our only choice should be to die
> Into that rest, or out of it.

For Berry, Sabbath is a reminder that his mind (his imagination) is cultivated by the Spirit of God, something that he cannot contain or control. Like Shaw, he chooses to submit his imagination to the One who is greater than he. For these artists, their work is done in submission to God, receiving from God.

The stereotype of administrative work includes endlessly responding to emails with corporate-speak clichés, soul-deadening spreadsheets, and mind-numbing meetings outlining processes that nobody needs or cares about. If, however, there were a way to infuse new perspectives into administrative work, is there hope of redemption? If we could develop an administrative imagination to help us make sense of our organizational ecosystems, if we are convinced that God is intimately involved in our work and our formation, I think everything could change.

As we delve more deeply into imagination in the context of administration in the next chapter, even this brief description of imagination suggests how catalytic imagination can be for administrators. If imagination is about helping us see our way forward, administrators need it because our job is to steward people, resources, and projects through a process—we need to have an idea about the end of the process in order to care well along the way. If imagination is about giving us new perspectives and helping us make sense of our world, we need it to be wise administrators to empathize well, putting together all the pieces so that we keep things both steady and moving forward. Finally, if imagination is about submitting to and receiving from God as an expression of wisdom, our posture in administration is the same—our way is directed by God.

# 10

# Imagination at Work

When I first started working in higher education administration, I would come to my supervisor with various issues that confounded me. I would lay out the players and the situation and suggest that we do option A or option B. He listened, usually asked a couple of questions, and then asked about option C . . . or option D . . . or option E, and so on. He was always kind, but this situation deeply annoyed me. I wanted to apprehend the variety of potential solutions rather than just settle for the bifurcated choices I brought to him. I was envious of his ability to perceive multiple options. I was seeing in black and white when I could have been seeing in color. I wanted to become a different kind of administrator. Thus began my journey toward administrative imagination.

Administrative work feels at its core to be all about solving problems—whether current problems presenting as such, or planning and organizing in hopes of avoiding problems in the future. The problems are big or small, deeply painful or moderately frustrating. Problem solving works best when we avoid just slotting in solutions that have been sufficient in the past but understand the ecosystem and name a spectrum of potential solutions in order to collaboratively land on the best way forward. This approach leads to a greater potential for the organization and its stakeholders to flourish.

The basic idea of imagination is "picturing to oneself." While this is foundational to how we function in the world, it's an easy capacity to overlook. Let's explore a familiar passage of Scripture with the lens to see how it speaks to this human function.

> [1]My child, do not forget my teaching,
> but let your heart keep my commandments,
> [2]for they will provide a long and full life,
> and well-being for you.
> [3]Do not let mercy and truth leave you;
> bind them around your neck,
> write them on the tablet of your heart.
> [4]Then you will find favor and good understanding,
> in the sight of God and people.
> [5]Trust in the LORD with all your heart,
> and do not rely on your own understanding.
> [6]Acknowledge him in all your ways,
> and he will make your paths straight.
> [7]Do not be wise in your own estimation;
> fear the LORD and turn away from evil.
> [8]This will bring healing to your body,
> and refreshment to your inner self. (Proverbs 3:1–8)

In the book of Proverbs, the concept of wisdom is overwhelmingly expressed in images and metaphors that provide us with clarity and helpful understanding of the kind of life into which following God's ways leads us. This passage exhorts us to remember God's teaching and to be obedient. Doing so leads to a life of flourishing, growth, and well-being.

Using images and personifying aspects of ourselves draw us into the writer's vision for faithfully walking with Yahweh. He suggests that the antidote to our forgetfulness of the ways of God is to bring our emotions and desires to the process, not just our minds. The experience of obedience is holistic, including our obedient hearts (v. 1). His next image in verse 3 is of permanently attaching love and faithfulness (such as the kind Yahweh exhibits toward his people). They are to be like a precious necklace we never remove. They are to be inscribed permanently on our heart. The writer assures us that keeping God's commands and God's ways close to us will lead to joy and delight, as well as an excellent life.

If we follow God, then there will be length of days, years of life, peace, favor, good success before God and man, straight paths, healing and refreshment for our bones. What a list! Even though verse 3 notes that it will go well with us if we keep love and faithfulness close, this is not an automatic guarantee in life. If it were, the exhortation to trust in the Lord with all our heart in verse 5 would be superfluous. Instead, the writer exhorts us to faith in God and to follow his ways, rather than our own. The result of this way of wisdom is healing and refreshment. The world in which we live is complicated and full of danger and evil. The antidote to that reality is holding unshakably to the things of God.

Proverbs call us to enter into this imaginative Christian life—to envision what following God and obeying his ways lead us into. It's an invitation to well-being, freedom, and joy. As we welcome God to fill our imagination, we find ourselves in a new place. Isaiah 43:19 describes what this can feel like:

> "Behold, I am doing a new thing;
> now it springs forth, do you not perceive it?
> I will make a way in the wilderness
> and rivers in the desert." (ESV)

This is God miraculously developing our organizational ecosystems to bring hope and life to the world.

### *Imaginative Administration*

Let's look at some of the foundational ways imagination is used in administration.

First, in administrative work, we often have disparate information, perspectives, and goals that need integrating. It takes imagination to see that X and Y belong together and an implication of that is Z—we have to paint a picture in words for others as we construct our arguments and persuade them of our perspectives and positions. The work of envisioning is imaginative. Because administrators have that mantle of stewarding people, resources, and projects through a process, we may see the end while others have yet to get there. We hold in view both the end and the path needed to get there. Our privilege is to invite others to see with us. Maybe we are the people who review feedback from stakeholders, and because we oversee processes, we have the opportunity to tweak and improve. Not all feedback is always welcomed, but being able to integrate stakeholder perspectives into suggestions for practical improvements requires a kind of imaginative seeing. Developing communication through our imaginative seeing provides the opportunity to bring others into seeing differently. This is foundational to the practice of administrative imagination.

Second, we need imagination to comprehend the complex problems that are part of our organizational ecosystems. When we encounter something that is not working, rarely can we change one variable and then be done with it. More often, we fix that variable and then find there is another affected area and another change for which we need to account. Administrative imagination allows us to grasp the ripple effects because it's not just one pebble thrown into the pond but a whole handful. Administrative imagination requires us to see the potential implications of change, as well as hold those effects until the context is prepared and the system has adequately absorbed the change.

At my church our faithful boiler had enough last November and gave up, so we entered the New England winter without heat in our building. This created a bevy of problems, which our leadership approached head-on. We moved from our glorious and impressive sanctuary to our run-of-the-mill church basement—it looks exactly as you are probably picturing it. The number of problems (or potential problems) with this move was impressive. Our leaders thought about everything from sourcing space heaters to ensuring that the candles, cross, and copy of the Scriptures in our processional, which are normally held high as they are brought into the worship space, would not scrape the much-lower ceiling. We changed the congregation's physical orientation—normally we sit facing north, but because of where the restrooms are, we now face south. Of great personal concern to me, as someone who serves with the kids, was that, because the children's classroom was now adjacent to the altar, should any of the toddlers have a meltdown or escape, the whole congregation would experience that. I'm so grateful for imaginative and adaptable leaders who have reenvisioned our worship space and will help us reflect well on this season of our church body and the opportunity for God's unique formation of us.

Third, we also need to imagine how our organizations can continue to develop in a healthy manner. When we can see aspects of our future context and bring it into where we are now, we can better prepare for a future that is still veiled. We need to find solutions to problems we've never encountered before. If those solutions end up being unhealthy to us, or to others, harm is caused—often irreversibly. In an ecosystem, if adjustments end up being destructive, the results can be catastrophic. Perhaps this is most clearly seen in hiring in organizations—individuals brought on in hopes that growth will occur. Often churches will hire a children's or youth pastor in hopes it will bring families to the community, and the finances may not be adequate to support that position yet.

It's easy to feel like administrative work is too restrictive for "true" imagination. There are seemingly endless limits of budgets, human resources, and time. However, the presence of boundaries provides opportunities to engage our imaginative capacities in greater measure than without those boundaries. This can feel counterintuitive, but think about the difference between a one-acre garden and a common two-feet-by-eight-feet garden plot. More creative capacity is required of us when greater boundaries are present. The difficulty present with greater boundaries invites us to a more intense practice of our imaginative capacity. Boundaries are certainly frustrating, but their presence does not prohibit the cultivation of fruitfulness of all kinds.

So, how do we develop our imaginative capacities? To know how to grow, we need to begin with a solid understanding of the kind of imaginer we are. Are you a "blue sky" thinker? Are you someone who tinkers? Do you need a narrative to write in your head to plan your next creative route? Can you just intuit things? Do you need to talk your ideas out to get to the imaginative part? Do you need to be aware of all the options available to you to maintain a sense of freedom?

One interesting way to get at this is to think about the kind of play that you liked to engage in as a child. A friend of mine loved Playmobil when she was younger. Playmobils are sets of small toys—little people and objects—designed in a variety of settings and around a variety of themes. She would build worlds out of her sets, making sense of a pirate set coupled with a jungle set, for example. She similarly does that in her work as an administrator, pulling together all the disparate needs and goals and then fostering a "world" in her organization that makes sense.

I was an "I wonder" kind of child—I'd have an idea and then play it out in my head to see if it was possible. My favorite spot was the hill behind our house—I'd lie down in this little divot in the grass, look at the sky, and just enjoy wherever my mind took me. I do that now as an administrator (although without the joy of lying in a field)—I wonder about giving a coworker a new responsibility or how a structural change might make things flow better. I wonder how a student might respond if I encourage them to think about a new option for their formation for ministry. The expression of wonder I began decades ago helps me envision various futures, facilitating better planning and decision making for me. As we name how we imagine, we can intentionally set aside time and space to do what used to come more naturally to us as children. A couple of categories for how we practice our imagination are described in the tool-kit section of this chapter.

Naming things about ourselves helps provide meaning, giving explanatory power to why we do what we do in the way that we do it. As Christians, we have the privilege of purposeful existence on Earth: we belong to the kingdom of God and have kingdom work to do in our jobs, with our families, with our neighbors, in whatever space we inhabit. That's similar to how we understand imagination in administration—we need to imagine our way through projects and processes, through relationships and seasons, and name who we are and how we do that in this process.

Time and the right kind of space are needed for fostering imagination. Growing our imaginative capacity generally will facilitate our administrative imagination specifically. Some of the best ways to grow imagination are to engage with art, poetry and fiction, and podcasts and stories from people not like us. Reading in disparate genres grows our vocabulary and our integrative capacity. Ideally, find time and space each week for your brain to be refreshed in creating something—bake bread, paint a picture, write a poem, do Sudoku—something that works a different part of your brain and uses another kind of creativity. Also, boredom is important for our imagination to be engaged. See what happens if you give yourself an hour to be bored—no tasks can be worked on, no entertainment engaged in, just boredom.[1]

Community is exceptionally helpful in developing our imaginative capacities. The gift of surrounding ourselves with others who are imaginative is a privilege. Invite conversation and wonder with a variety of people to test your ideas and increase your imaginative input. One of the unexpected joys for me during the season of COVID happened on Thursday evenings. My friends Jeff and Teal gathered a group of us on the outdoor patio of a local brewery. We spent a couple of hours each week hearing interesting stories from others, batting about various questions about ourselves and the world, testing hypotheses, and having fun. The space and time that season offered us bore dividends in imaginative capacity development for all of us. We found ourselves changed through the practice of wondering together. The confidence provided by others can be a really helpful catalyst to our imaginative process. Specifically for development of imagination for administration, having conversations with others who see through that lens with those convictions is uniquely valuable.

### *Tool Kit: Imagining Together*

Sometimes the attempt to bring imaginers together feels like a cacophony rather than a symphony. This tool kit is about how to create the kind of environment where strengths are played to and people can practice what they do best. After describing several kinds of imagination, we will look at creating an environment where they can be practiced together. These categories are from JoAnn Franklin Klinker, who writes about imagination in higher education administration.[2]

*Descriptive imagination* "identifies patterns and visualizes what is indefinable." If you are in a conversation that includes disparate arguments and points of view, and someone pulls everything together to make sense of what's been said, that takes imagining the thing the conversation has become. It requires integrating it all and describing it, which creates meaning. People with descriptive imagination paint pictures of what the rest of us cannot see yet. A key skill for this is employing metaphors.

*Creative imagination* "transforms existing concepts." That's something new that we've never seen before in our context. The people who do this turn the descriptive imaginings into something else. It's the person who comes after the clarification who says, "what if we did *this*" (and the "this" is something new). They excel at innovation. People with creative imagination are the ones the rest of us look at and think, "Wow—I never would have thought of that in a million years!"

The final category, *challenging imagination,* is "critically evaluating the progress made from the previous imaginings." It takes discernment, but also "seeing" the potential result and evaluating it. One using challenging imagination often revisits or refreshes the other two categories as a "bridge between theory and practice."[3] This is the person who takes what is new and can visualize the potential problems and concerns needing to be addressed—they integrate the idea into the context and create meaning by putting some feet on it. The timing of this kind of imagining is important because some members of the team might not be ready for the challenge yet. They have not fully apprehended the concepts or the new thing yet, and they don't get the chance to live into the potential before the eager challenger comes along and reorients everyone. The challenger may need coaching on when and how to speak up—they need to do their very important job empathetically. People with challenging imagination are the ones the rest of us look at and think, "Wow, you just saved us a whole lot of time and money that would have been wasted otherwise!"

Given that people usually fall into one (or more) of these categories, let's talk through how to create an environment where these can be expressed.

Creating space for the people with descriptive imagination skills might look like waiting in silence for the internal processors to do what they need to do. It might look like having a premeeting with a key describer so they can be thinking ahead of time. It might be giving people paper and markers to pictorially represent what has been said in the meeting. Let's say you want to develop an event to help your people learn about and grow in their spiritual disciplines. You might open the meeting with some exploratory questions: ask people to describe a life-changing experience they had practicing a spiritual discipline. Ask about their most significant memory from youth group or a retreat, etc. The person with descriptive imagination will hopefully be able to take those threads and stories and weave a shared picture or vision.

To foster space for the people who have creative imagination might require more intentional setting of place and feel. It might mean giving time for people to work out the transformative concepts they intuit. And it might mean making sure people have the resources to do so—from paper and markers to software and Google. This may mean planning a follow-up meeting or creating time for triads to discuss things. In our example, maybe once you have that picture of experiences related to spiritual disciplines, this person can translate that into your particular context. Maybe this person can help the team visualize what a ministry retreat would feel like, building and creating something never before experienced in your context.

The people who bring challenging imagination need to know that when they provide needed critique, their positions or influence in the organization will not change with this gift they bring. If they give a green light, that doesn't mean they get favor. If they give a red light, that doesn't mean their job is at stake. They need to be assured that their truthfulness is expected. This is the person who asks questions about affordability, child care, location, and other aspects of feasibility, including whether something is needed at all. The person will ask about felt needs and how you will know what success means within this new venture.

Undergirding all the tools required for imaginative expression is psychological and emotional health. If a team member's mental health is deteriorating, that will affect how we can imagine together. Anxiety can seep into the dynamic of the group and curtail generative ideas, for example, or an insecure leader may be tempted to place restrictive limits on someone who excels in one kind of imaginative expression. There are many ways a healthy group dynamic can be sabotaged, so paying close attention and listening well in order to help the group get on better footing is a key task for leader and members.

All three of these roles are needed on a team, and each is valuable. We must cultivate the space to ensure that everyone can practice these with permission and freedom. Coming up with new and good ideas that will last takes time and space. Be organized and plan well, but also be flexible and change course. Being aware of the kind of imagining we tend toward allows us to see how we may affect others. If you are comfortable in challenging, that may put a damper on the creative people. If you live in the descriptive area, the other two folks might feel like you never want to go beyond just knowing a good definition of the thing you are working on. Developing the way we practice our imagination invites a beautifully integrative expression of gifts leading to much joy!

### *Questions for Reflection*

1. In what ways does administration require imagination in your experience?
2. How did you play and use your imagination when you were a child? Are those themes reflected in your current administrative work?
3. What examples have you seen of people who are imaginative in an administrative context? How have they influenced you?
4. What kind of an imagination do you tend to practice in your organizational ecosystem? How do you see that affecting others around you as you seek to "take good care"?

11

# Design Thinking for Administrators

This chapter is entirely a tool kit. We are going to map out the process of design thinking for administrators in an organizational ecosystem.

Design thinking is simply the ability to innovate with empathy. Innovation is about figuring out a new way to do something, and empathy is understanding the experience of others. Design thinking, therefore, is figuring out new ways to solve problems while being attentive to others.

Design thinking is a wonderful tool that allows us to image our loving Creator. Creation ex nihilo—out of nothing—is impossible for us, so we dwell in the world of innovation. We are invited into a life of love for this diverse world we inhabit, echoing the posture of a gracious and self-giving God. Design thinking allows for both worship of our loving Creator and delight in the work he invites us into, following in his footsteps in some way.

In 1979 industrial designer Patricia Moore (who was twenty-six at the time) began to dress like and live as an elderly woman to experience the world as seniors do. She ended up creating helpful designs for all sorts of products, some of which became staples in the OXO brand of kitchen tools. If you are not familiar with OXO, these products are usually the best-feeling ones out there. I will never buy another brand of can opener besides OXO again. Moore is often regarded as the mother of universal design. What she did in dressing up as an elderly woman is emblematic of design thinking because she literally put on the shoes of her end user. Her commitment to solving problems for the elderly was innovation with empathy.

Even before Patricia Moore, design thinking as a process began in the late '50s and early '60s in the world of engineering. Designers started using "mock-up environments" and ethnographic field research. In the '80s, design thinking began flourishing in the world of architecture, partially due to Moore. A key player in the last thirty years of design thinking has been the design firm IDEO, which was started in the early '90s.[1] Stanford professor David M. Kelley built the firm on these principles: they (1) seek to understand the market; (2) observe real people in real-life situations; (3) visualize the concepts and the people who will use them; (4) evaluate and refine the prototypes; and (5) implement the new concept.[2] From working on the electric version of the Ford F-150, to developing digital resources for youth mental health, to redesigning the Sephora beauty care experience, to having the community in Frisco, Texas, design Grand Park (an urban oasis), IDEO applies their principles to a spectrum of opportunities.[3]

One of my favorite developments of design thinking in a new area came out of Stanford's design school—Bill Burnett and Dave Evans developed a college course at Stanford about finding your calling and vocation based on design thinking. The course became a book called *Designing Your Life*, and then *Designing Your New Work Life* as well.[4] The class that started at Stanford came out of Dave Evans wanting to help students find meaning in their work, since he heard from them that issues of vocation were huge. The problem he observed was people floundering in figuring out what they could do in their lives. The answer was to employ design thinking to solve that problem. Instead of picking a job that fit their major (which itself may not have been chosen for meaningful reasons), students were invited to envision what they wanted their lives to be all about, and then the process reverse-engineers back from that picture.

Administrative challenges in an organizational ecosystem are the perfect context for design thinking. After looking at the basic building blocks for design thinking (empathy, integration, and the right tools), we will explore a process for using it.

Empathy often arises out of our imagination, when we try to see the world through someone else's eyes. If the goal is to keep the end user in mind as we problem-solve, to the best of our ability, we need to be able to understand that person or population. Empathy is sharing joy when a coworker receives a raise and frustration when plans crumble. We use empathy every day, every hour, and in every email we send in our work with people. Especially when we look at problems, perceiving how others experience them is crucial—they may not even see an issue, or things may be far more difficult for them than we initially thought.

The second building block is integration. Integration is about seeing the whole. Design thinking puts together the experiences of the end user—the raw material needed, the process of the makers, the social and cultural implications, and more. Using integrative thought allows us to put together systems and processes in order for our solution to actually work. Suppose it's time to overhaul a training process. We would begin with the end user, including all the people and information (raw materials) needed to get to the end user, and then think about the system, the culture—everything that eventually goes into that learning experience. Integration requires holding a lot of things simultaneously, intentionally acknowledging the relationships that exist, and inviting even more of those connections.

The third foundation for design thinking is having the right tools, which, in this case, are the right mind-sets and skill sets necessary. To do design thinking we need to ensure that our minds are oriented in particular ways and that we have the skills to do the designing needed. But first, let's shift to the administration context as we explore appropriate mind-sets. The first question we need to answer is: Who is our end user? Even before we name our problem, we need to know:

"Who is this education for?"
"Who is our church for?"
"Who is this nonprofit for?"

There is not a wrong answer, but there ideally is a requirement for agreement on the identity of the end user among the stakeholders. Our mission, as well as our implicit culture, should provide direction for this. To whom do stakeholders refer when they talk about why you are doing what you are doing? What kinds of artifacts do you have around that give clues about this question? It's important to be honest (and not idealistic or necessarily theologically correct) about who our end user is. Once we have that piece sorted, we create some boundaries, and boundaries create opportunities from which innovation can rise. Think of what your boundaries might be related to this question. Push the boundary out as far as you can. Sometimes when we are solving these problems, it's helpful to have multiple end users—maybe an immediate one like a student, parishioner, city, etc., but also an ultimate one for the whole enterprise (the church, God, etc.).

We need to get ourselves in the right frame of mind to do design thinking. What are those ways of thinking? What follows comes out of my experience and research as I've engaged with imaginative administrators. First, we need a strong sense of curiosity, developing the practice of wonder. Curiosity is cultivated and is a discipline. It relies on sharpening our observational abilities and our skills related to asking questions that may not have ready-made answers. One of the best ways to grow curiosity is to hang around people who are curious. Maybe that's following some artists or inventors on Instagram. Maybe that's having an agenda-less lunch with some friends with whom you can just toss out a topic and wonder together about it. (You could start small, like, "What does it mean to be truly human these days?") Journaling also helps with understanding as we trammel those observations through reflection.

We also need imaginative capacity to see the whole (which is integrative meaning making—see chapter 8 for more on that). The final mind-set is a bias to action. Practically, that means saying yes until we have to say no (see the tool kit for chapter 5 for an in-depth explanation). This pushes back against the "head in the clouds" stereotype imaginative people often have. When we are designing, we prototype, we try things out. Bias to action gives us energy to do that. It's the stance that helps us go!

In addition to mind-sets, design thinking also requires a skill set. To walk through the skills of design thinking, let's use an illustration—suppose you want to address a concern related to church visitors who are not turning into members. What skills do we need to employ design thinking to solve that problem?

The first skill is to ask questions to understand the real problem, to develop awareness. This is about leaving our presuppositions at the door. IDEO suggests that we frame our concern as a question that begins with "how might we . . ." and then ask the question behind the concern. So, for our example, our question could be "How might we build an effective ministry to young adults so they join our church?" At this point, the answer to that question could be anything from getting new furniture to overhauling the curriculum/sermon content. Note that this skill connects with the mind-set of *curiosity*—the skill is asking the right question, the mind-set is the curiosity to do so. Learning to ask good questions is the same as learning curiosity—we hang around people who do that well, pay attention, and practice! When we are doing administrative work, we usually have a sense of what the problem generally is: How do I get this person to perform differently? how can this be more efficient? what's the matter with this process? However, broad brushstrokes are insufficient to get us anywhere actionable because we get overwhelmed at the complexity. "How might we get 500,000 more young adults to join us?" is not helpful for what we want to do with design thinking. Asking the question more narrowly and with more focus is going to get us closer to a solution. For example: "How might we better train our community to engage with young adults when we are unfamiliar with them and have difficulty relating?" is probably going to get us somewhere. The problem that is *solvable* is not really that we lack the right ministry plans (we might eventually discover that), but it might be insufficient training, lack of social skills, or wrong assumptions about young people. Those are problems we can address.

This leads us to the second skill: communicating to frame the problem. What is the message at the heart of the problem? How will you share the message multiple times and in multiple ways so other people care about your question as much as you do? That requires using all of our communication to talk about it, to develop shared language and practices. With our example, talking about young adults might be anything from five minutes at a staff meeting giving tips on what to do when you are chatting with a young person, to emails to your community with encouragement to engage young adults, to positive reinforcement when you see that happening, etc. The skill of communication coordinates well with the mind-set of *imagination* for administrators. Integrative meaning making—describing, creating, and challenging—requires effective communication for the sake of solving the problem with others.

The third skill is radical collaboration, or partnership, to solve the problem. Everyone needs to help solve these kinds of broad problems. Working with young adults should never just be confined to a particular staff member or designated volunteer. It's about everyone—the folks who are just around—people who walk the halls regularly. We must engage in collaboration unlike we've ever had to before. This partners well with *bias to action*—we are always moving forward in our work, poised to go together.

Now that we've looked at what design thinking is, and what skill sets and mind-sets are required, let's walk through the process. Design thinking should not feel overwhelmingly complicated because there is a logical progression. After explaining the seven steps, the process will then be illustrated with a subsequent example. The steps are as follows:

1. Be clear on what the problem really is: "How might we . . . ?"
2. Name who the solution is for and why they need it. You've named your end user (or users), and you need to make sure they are connected to the problem and solution in a clear way. Remember the story of the medieval lord who surveyed workers about what they

were doing—are you a bricklayer or a worshiper who gets to build a cathedral?

3. Brainstorm—find lots of ideas, impractical and conventional! The joy of radical collaboration is probably best seen here. Catalysts to creativity happen on this step.
4. Categorize the kinds of solutions—put stuff that is alike in a bucket. This is just a general organizational tool to help you grasp what you have to potentially work with.
5. Discern which category best addresses the end user's situation, keeping in mind the raw materials available. This is the part where you come down from the clouds into the real world a little more.
6. Describe what tools are needed within that category. Think about money, time, people, skill sets, etc.
7. "Make it work" with the best solution . . . and then iterate. Iteration requires creating room for failure financially and psychologically.

Here's an illustration from the institution where I work. Several years ago, our students were requesting a high number of end-of-semester extensions to get their work done. This overwhelmed the registration office, as they evaluated those requests. Students could take a grade reduction in exchange for a couple of extra days when it was not an emergency (they were given extra time with no penalty in cases of actual emergency). As we started looking at this, it became clear the problem was not really too many extensions. We needed a way to change the culture of procrastination and unhelpful study habits coupled with the lack of planning we were observing. Students were using this as a crutch and not changing their study habits to avoid these extensions. The "how might we" question in our design thinking process ended up being, "How might we help our students build different time-management and life-balancing skills?" Our solution was to change the policy so only "unforeseen circumstances and emergencies" are considered for extensions. We moved the evaluation responsibility to Student Life instead of Registration because we in Student Life had more time capacity, and it allowed us another avenue into student care and support. The key to advocating for this change and unlocking a better solution was our recognition that the end user is not the student or faculty but the future context for our students (such as a church or organization). This was who we needed to serve in this situation. We needed to help our students avoid a rhythm of taking a grade reduction for simple time mismanagement or poor planning. For our students training to be pastors, Sunday morning comes whether they are ready or not. However, we also wanted them to experience a culture of grace and support when emergencies happen. Part of our solution also included doing more education and training for our students on organization and study planning.

In short, we . . .

1. Named who the solution was for—future contexts of work and ministry.
2. Asked how might we . . . help our students develop different planning and time-management skills.
3. Brainstormed (this consisted of a conversation between the registrar and dean of students).
4. Categorized . . . policy change (no more grade reductions) and a process change (going to Student Life), as well as learning opportunities (workshops).
5. Discerned which category and solution worked best. We looked at what was possible with the process and timeline we had available. Faculty needed to buy into this change, the handbook needed updating, and we had to time the changes so that students had adequate runway to adapt to this change.
6. Used collaboration and communication as our main tools. The registrar provided training and guidance. She was always willing to help sort out complex situations that arose with student requests.
7. And later figured out how to deal with January term timing; we made sure we were serving our students with academic accommodations well; and we managed other issues as they arose.

Four years in, we are happy with this solution, and the number of extensions has decreased overall. We call our process of design thinking and the solution that resulted a success!

In closing, here is a blessing on this process and all the potential fruit we hope it brings forth:

> May the God of all creativity and wonder give you wisdom and insight as you serve him in the work that he has given you to do. May you see his love as you solve problems, and may he guide you into solutions beyond what you could ask or imagine.

### *Questions for Reflection*

1. How do you describe yourself as a problem solver? What is your greatest strength as you think about how you would practice design thinking?
2. What mind-sets or skill sets will be easier for you to employ than others?
3. What mind-sets or skill sets will be more difficult for you to employ than others?
4. What kinds of things would be challenges to using design thinking in your context?
5. To what current problems could you apply design thinking?

# Part 5

## *Administration in* Memento Mori

A college pastor I once worked with announced on his first day that he was planning on staying at the church until he died. We are the same age, and I remember being both impressed at his sense of commitment and skeptical of the wisdom of his pronouncement. He left after less than two years. The senior pastor of that church had also told us that he planned on staying there until he retired. He has indeed been at the same church for twenty-eight years and counting. Tenure in a particular organizational ecosystem varies according to many factors, and each participant's stay affects the whole in some way. In a biological ecosystem, processes are present so that death has the potential to contribute to the flourishing of others. We ought to seek replication of that kind of flourishing in our organizational ecosystems.

Some people are able to maintain a very clear perspective on how long they are going to stay at a particular position. If their progress through the ranks does not result in promotion at the right time, they are happy to find a job elsewhere. A friend of mine is an expert in changing jobs—he had five positions in ten years, each a promotion with a higher salary and better context than the last.

Tenure trends tend to fall in interesting generational lines. Boomers stay in their positions on average 8 years, 3 months;

Gen Xers stay 5 years, 2 months; millennials, 2 years, 9 months; and Gen Zers, 2 years, 3 months.[1] Overall the tenure of the workforce in the United States is 3.9 years (as of 2024).[2] That's a challenging dynamic for organizations to navigate without having both an accurate expectation of turnover and the tools and mechanisms to foster smooth transitions.

One approach to setting ourselves and our organizations up for thriving in this reality is "administration in *memento mori*," or administration remembering our death. We ought not to treat people who leave organizations as if they had died, but sometimes the practical effect on the work is similar—an abrupt transition in a project is needed because someone surprisingly gives their two-week notice. Institutional memory is lost because someone has an emergency surgery and cannot come back to work. Someone is out of pocket because their family has a crisis and they rightly put them first. Deaths that blindside us occur as well.

The concept of *memento mori* arises most often during the season of Lent, the time in the church calendar where we are encouraged to remember our own death, moving toward Good Friday as we reflect on Jesus's crucifixion. Remembering that we are dust and to dust we will return is the center point of Ash Wednesday, providing us with a helpful trajectory on the entire Lenten season. During Ash Wednesday services, as the priest takes ashes and makes a cross on our foreheads, "*memento mori*" is an exhortation to think deeply about our life now in light of the certainty of death.

What if we were to take a similar perspective to our administrative work in organizations? How would that give us perspective and focus on what we do and how we do it? We have no idea how long our tenure will be at our current organization—it may encompass the entirety of our working life, or it may be one stop among many in an itinerant professional career. Regardless of how long our stay ends up being, how can we bring the perspective of our own eventual death into our organization so that life and growth come? It's an unexpected approach that leads us into a place of flourishing for ourselves and our organizations.

In the next chapter we will explore "nestedness," a way of being found in many ecosystems, and look at what is needed for this particular approach to withstand crises and stress, with resilience as the goal. After that we will look at succession planning and feedback loops, as we recognize the life cycle of organizations. Preparing for movement into key positions requires our formation as we attend to our engagement in particular stages in our organization. Finally, we will reflect on investing beyond our years, keeping kingdom perspective in our work. Administrative work in *memento mori* invites us to plan a certain way, taking a certain kind of perspective that is often lost in the day-to-day.

The ashen cross inscribed in our foreheads on Ash Wednesday is also an unexpected hint toward hope and life. Often churches will save the palm branches from the previous year's celebration of Jesus as the triumphant King coming to Jerusalem on Palm Sunday, burn the branches, and then use that as the ashes. Death is certain, and that tie to Jesus, our King who came to Earth, died, was buried, and rose again, reminds us that his life is ours as well. We will also die, be buried, and raised to new life again.

That changes everything.

# 12

# Nestedness

When I was in seminary, I attended a church that planted a campus in a town about thirty minutes away from our main location. I interned at the church while this work was happening, so I had the privilege of attending staff meetings where the newly hired campus pastor, the executive pastor, and the lead pastor worked out the vision for this plant. The idea was to develop this location as a site of the church, but contextualized to the people who lived in this town.

There were many cues denoting that the satellite campus was connected to the main campus. The logo was the same. The bulletin was the same. The music was the same style. When I attended services at both locations on the same morning, it was always striking to me that the two preachers (who were *very* different individuals) could take the same passage and preach it with the same main points, using different illustrations and applications. It usually worked! Some Sundays it felt like we were playing a game of telephone where the original message is passed along, but we caught it early enough to discern the original intent.

All the small-group leaders at the church were trained in the same way, with the same vision and values, which was my responsibility when my internship turned into a staff position. The majority of the groups even used the same curriculum since we had a teaching-team model where one of the pastors planned out each sermon series with passages and main points. Then I would use that content to develop a curriculum for the small-group leaders. When I visited groups, the discussions were similar but varied depending on who was in each group.

The goal of all of this replication and intentionality in keeping the DNA of the church consistent was to develop a resilient organization.[1] When a good portion of the staff went on a mission trip over the summer, when the lead pastor went on sabbatical, when the teaching pastor moved away, we were able to continue living into the vision that had been set out. The technical term for what we were doing (in ecosystem lingo) was creating "nestedness."

Nestedness is a structure in which similar versions of the same species occur iteratively as a means of protecting biodiversity. One way to visualize nestedness is to imagine a series of islands radiating out from a primary one. That main island has a rich and diverse expression of species, flora, and fauna—from large to microscopic. Then, imagine the next island out—it will have some of the species of the main island but is smaller and has additional special features due to its unique size and topography. The third island out is even smaller, and it also replicates some aspects of the first two islands, with a little variation of its own. Nestedness allows for resiliency of species because, if there's a catastrophic event on the main island, all is not lost because of what has occurred on the subsequent islands emanating out.

Nestedness builds redundancy, which fosters resilience in species and in ecosystems overall. When subsets are present in other locations, this provides capacity for a variety of changes, especially in the case of perturbation (a term that refers to "external induced shock").[2] This provides flexibility and capacity for survival. Scientists also point to another dynamic of ecosystem nestedness whereby "specialists tend to interact with generalists rather than with other specialists."[3] This way if a specialist is removed from the system, things do not collapse right away because the generalists understand what is going on. Other species adapt and fill in if a particular specialized species is removed.

### *Nestedness and Administration*

For organizations, nestedness provides a similar measure of health and overall well-being. When organizations are able to maintain mission, culture, and even tasks for the locations, departments, and offices emanating out, it is more likely the organization will survive a large-scale catastrophe and even smaller-scale change.

For administrators, nestedness can be a huge headache. Depending on the structure of the organization, it can mean double the work, double the trouble. Nestedness done well may mean more tasks, including ensuring that others are cross-trained, but it can also lead to an organization that is resilient and flourishes in a beautiful way. Sometimes we are tempted to structure ourselves as silos for the sake of efficiency. Why should someone else learn aspects of my job when they can be freed to do their thing? Nestedness can feel like a waste of time and energy. Organizations that are nested tend to be stronger overall because participants are familiar with what others do and thus capable of filling in at times.

At my friend Amber's church, she and another member filled in for a staff member on maternity leave, each taking responsibility for aspects of the job. When the staff member came back, the ministry was stronger than it had been several months previously because more people were deeply invested and able to lead. Nestedness means when the unexpected happens, operations do not crumble, but others can build up around the person who was directly affected. The ecosystem is not devastated overall but has the space and time to adapt due to cross-training. When specialists and generalists engage with each other, developing competencies in multiple spaces, the organization as a whole has a greater chance for survival. Organizations will always need specialists, but expanding everyone's capacities for generalism is a worthwhile endeavor.

In higher education, nestedness is an incredibly important aspect of our goal to serve students well. It's not enough for Student Life to be experts at only the work we do in our department, but the system as a whole depends on Student Services[4] staff members to have a level of familiarity with the policies and processes of other departments. When we neglect to learn more or provide incorrect information, the student is negatively affected, which may affect their ability to complete their degree. For example, suppose a student comes to me in Student Life with a question about their eligibility for an end-of-semester extension due to experiencing depression following the recent death of their parent. The student may just ask for an extra three days extension on an assignment at the end of the semester, but I also have the opportunity to invite them to consider the next semester's schedule and how the particular courses they are planning on taking may not give them space to grieve. I can suggest a couple of alternatives and remind them that a change in credit hours could impact their financial aid eligibility. I can review registration policies with them so they know their options and the timeline for withdrawing to receive a refund, while also encouraging them to connect with Financial Aid and Registration along the way as they are making this decision. I'll also suggest they take the opportunity to receive counseling and possibly connect them with a faculty member for additional guidance. If, however, I were to just stick to the areas in which I am a specialist (approving the extension request), I have not served the student well, nor have I been a helpful member of the ecosystem overall.

Within a biological ecosystem, keystone species are those organisms for which the entire system is dependent and, if they are removed, everything crumbles. Keystone actors in organizational ecosystems are those people in various strategic positions who hold crucial positions for the well-being of the whole. There might be a couple of keystone actors in an organization where, if something happens to them, implosion is imminent. Nestedness works to push back against that precariousness. The top leader may or may not be a keystone actor in an ecosystem—it is often healthier for the organization if the top leader does not have that role (and it's best if no one really has that role!). The next chapter examines how to provide a healthy transition for key administrators in organizations.

### *A Nested Early Church*

Functioning well in a nested organizational ecosystem necessitates certain kinds of administrative capabilities: influence, response to change, and adaptation.[5] As those tasked with stewarding people, resources, and projects through a process, administrators primarily express these capabilities. We'll look at the early church as a snapshot of incredibly successful nestedness, observing how the apostles shepherded these communities.

One of my favorite scenes to visualize from Scripture is the moment after Jesus ascended, the disciples just standing there, squinting at the sky, hearts pounding, looking at each other, befuddled at what they had just seen. I doubt any of them jumped in immediately with "Okay, fellas! Here's the four-step plan of how we are going to get this great commission off the ground!" They had been given their short-term plans: "Do not leave Jerusalem, but wait there for what my Father promised, which you heard about from me" (Acts 1:4), but the rest of it had yet to be unfolded.

The complex task of bringing the gospel to all the world was utterly dependent on the apostles being filled with the Holy Spirit, who would empower and lead them in this endeavor. After Peter's initial sermon on the day of Pentecost, when three thousand believed, there was a time of learning, community organization, and formation: "They were devoting themselves to the apostles' teaching and to fellowship, to the breaking of bread and to prayer" (Acts 2:42). They engaged with each other and with the leaders, and began the process of working out what they had accepted to be true about God. There were miracles and opposition, all of which were evidence that, even though Jesus was not bodily present, his power and love abounded through the presence of the Spirit.

After this period of time where initial converts were taught and formed in this new way in Jerusalem, it became apparent that the movement needed to expand outside of the city confines. Persecution was part of the reason for leaving—on the very day when Stephen testified so powerfully about the historical witness to Jesus, significant harassment, trouble, and torture broke out (Acts 8:1). The apostles kept Jerusalem as their home base for a little while as others spread throughout the area (Acts 8:1). Communities of learning and formation sprang up throughout the region (we call them churches). The apostles visited them regularly and even communicated via letters, addressing concerns and encouraging them to faithful obedience.

While Scripture does not directly address the administrative capabilities of the apostles (although administration is a gift of the Spirit), we can see that the foundational building blocks of administration in a nested organization are present (influence, response to change, and adaptation).

When silos are removed, seeing as much of the whole as possible is vital. Accompanying comprehensive sight is the need to develop appropriate influence. In Acts 8, Philip was directed to leave home base in Jerusalem (his previous silo) and head down toward Gaza, whereupon he met the Ethiopian eunuch. Philip explained Scripture to him, baptized him, and then was skirted away to Azotus. Philip's posture was to just go where the Lord sent him to bring the good news of the gospel, wherever that might be. He understood the overall mission, and the willingness to go wherever that took him fostered significant influence in his ministry.

According to Nicolai J. Foss and his colleagues, leadership in an ecosystem requires a "wide lens" or a "holistic, system-level perspective beyond the boundaries of one's firm," as well as prior experience upon which to build.[6] These two arms demonstrate a challenge, particularly when a response to change is warranted. It's not enough to simply be a visionary and to see that hoped-for reality coming out of a vacuum, but context and experience are vital in an ecosystem when it's time for a response to change.

Perhaps the most dramatic response to change in the early church was how they accepted Saul, their former persecutor, as a leader after he met Jesus on the road to Damascus. Ananias came close to this man and taught him, trusting the Lord and Saul that his conversion was real. Saul preached Jesus fearlessly and ended up as one of the key authorities of the early church. He corrected Peter, corrected the Corinthians (among other churches), and presented clear doctrine for acceptance by the church. His apostle colleagues must have experienced whiplash to go from seeing Saul as their enemy to seeing him as their leader. Somehow, by God's grace and through the resiliency of this newly formed organization, this was a successful response to change.

The church and its leaders not only accepted Saul (who later became known as Paul) and adapted to his leadership, but they also adapted to the ever-growing expansion of the church overall. They welcomed gentiles (see Peter's experience with Cornelius in Acts 10), sent members off on journeys to share the gospel and help establish churches (Acts 13; 16–20), contended with the established Jewish religious leaders and civil leaders (Acts 14; 19–26), clarified the mission of the church (Acts 15), and dealt with interpersonal conflict (Acts 15). While the story of Acts is told as the account of several key leaders, those who joined the movement of Christians mostly stayed where they were, adapting their daily and weekly rhythms, shifting the ways they engaged with neighbors, changing how they related to religious leaders, and perhaps addressing conflict with civil leaders, and more. Church history is replete with occurrences of adaptation for the church, even as it is firmly established in society. May God continue to guide through the centuries.

As organizations continue to develop structures and practices that contribute to nestedness—developing our influence, response to change, and adaptation—we as administrators will contribute to the creation of resilient organizations.

### *Tool Kit: Season Planning to Avoid Burnout*

The complexity of nestedness requires us to think well about time—not just daily or even weekly time management, but seasons of time. We cannot know the length of our days, so we ought to number them rightly (Psalm 90:12). Responsiveness to the ecosystem occurs across a spectrum, from minutiae to broad, sweeping changes. Different energy is required for season planning, and we do it less frequently than we do other kinds of time planning (we do daily and weekly planning much more frequently). We also live in a fast-paced and demanding world, where burnout is seemingly around every corner. Season planning contributes to healthy rhythms, which are an antidote to burnout.[7]

Sabbath is one of the most important practices for us as administrators.[8] Sabbath is the intentional ceasing of work for a period of time in order to worship. Doing so gives us perspective and a life-giving reset on who we are and what we are doing. Sabbath is also about engagement—with the Lord, community, and creation—all for the sake of joy. Normally, we practice Sabbath weekly and find times to cease our work seasonally as well. This is where season planning can be helpful as we evaluate means of restoration. Seasons give us a longer runway for reflection and evaluation. Midseason corrections can be really helpful, and end-of-season evaluations contribute to healthy iteration over the long haul.

Season planning includes looking ahead to a more significant chunk of time that contains a particular theme. The holiday season has more events and more details to plan compared to the quiet of midwinter when we want to cozy up on our couches with a book. In my work context, fall brings a lot of excitement and relationship-building work, but summer is a time for deep work, planning, and large-scale projects. Anticipating the season allows us to funnel resources wisely, preparing for an anticipated future. We can identify what is important to us and organize accordingly. Toward that goal, it can be helpful to ask ourselves what we will be disappointed with if we reach the end of the season and it has not happened. That gives us the focus for where our attention needs to be directed. It's easy to direct attention to things that do not really matter to us because we have not done the work of reflection, allowing us to prioritize wisely.

Below is a series of prompts and questions that can help us think about managing our seasonal energy wisely.

1. Be cognizant of your strengths as you are season planning.
    a. What aspects of your work do you find most enjoyable?
    b. What are your unique ways of working? When we name our

skills and abilities, it helps us understand why some kinds of work or projects cause less stress than others.

c. How have you named your calling so that it provides motivation along the way? I've seen students who have a picture of the country they are called to as a missionary posted on their library carrel, and that serves to focus their energy in their studies. If it feels difficult to name your calling, remember what brought you to your organization in the first place.

2. Pay attention to your preferred work flow. What helps you do your best work over a significant period of time?

As an illustration for how this works for me, I had the joy and challenge of getting my PhD while working full time. As you might imagine, this required a lot of planning and strategizing! I completed my PhD entirely before 8:00 a.m. Monday through Friday and on Saturdays. It took me five and a half years, which was a very long season! It was important to me to work full time both because of that particular job opportunity and because I wanted to avoid debt for my PhD. I know that, as a morning person, I lack energy to engage with ideas and writing in the evening, so that meant developing the discipline of going to bed early so I could get up early to study.

When it was time to figure out how to "project-manage" my dissertation, I developed some helpful tools. First, I'd email my dissertation advisor every Monday morning with a report on what I had done the previous week and a plan for what I was going to do that week. I told him he was not expected to actually read those emails, but I wanted the accountability of him *possibly* reading them. I like to visualize my assignments and tasks, so I'd often fill out monthly calendar sheets to schedule things out for the semester or stick posters on my wall to see the flow of small tasks to larger goals. A healthy rhythm over time leads to good results, as long as we are keeping what matters in mind and wisely building that rhythm.

Here are some considerations regarding work flow:

a. Time. When do you have the *right* energy for your most important work? Time is like a budget—you have a limited amount, so pay the priority bill first and then buy your Starbucks with what is left. Make sure you are thinking about what matters most in this season; if family is the thing that matters, figure out how to prioritize around that. The practice of wisdom in prioritizing our time is crucial to season planning, so constantly bringing our time before the Lord for his guidance allows us to work with a sense of freedom and abundance rather than bondage and scarcity.
b. Space. Where do you work best? Keep boundaries of what you do where to help your brain and body work together best to know when to work, when to rest, and when to play. This is about taking good care of ourselves because the right spatial boundaries can lead us into a state of flourishing.
c. Tools. It is so important to use a calendar, whether digital or paper. Use it to block time for projects and deadlines. Use a timer if focus is difficult to attain—try the Pomodoro method, which is twenty-five minutes on, five minutes off, etc. There are also tools to help us with the temptation of social media. Our need for tools can be a meaningful reminder of our finitude and fallenness—and the grace of good tools that help us in our limitations.
d. Contingencies. What happens when the optimal setup evades you? Maybe you are a parent, or illness occurs, etc. How do you name your disappointment and not obsess over what is less than ideal? Are you a perfectionist about this stuff? How will you manage yourself? What a wonderful opportunity to practice our sanctification!

3. Figure out your order of operations (get organized!).
   a. List your major projects/tasks/assignments. You are the person who is responsible for ensuring tasks get done in this season, and bringing this list to God in invitation to set your steps helps affirm God's place in your work.

b. Read through your list, making note of what needs to happen to get your tasks done. How long will it take you to accomplish them, generally speaking? What are the subtasks needed to accomplish the larger projects? God is present in the little things, reminding us of his love and care for us.

c. Create a workable timeline—use a calendar of some kind (either weekly, monthly, quarterly, or even yearly). Faith is always needed as we plan; since our understanding is limited, trusting the Lord will provide exactly what is needed at the right time.

    i. Begin with Sabbath. Trying to squeeze it in at the end will cheapen it.

    ii. Put in the anchors (events or due dates, for example).

    iii. Work backward with how much time you need to prep. Do this in pencil because adaptability is indispensable.

    iv. Front-load! Do more work than you need to earlier than necessary. Plan your quiet weeks wisely! Recognize the places where you may need to sacrifice. This is about choosing what matters to you. One caveat: It's really easy for an organization to foster a culture of cramming and, while a little bit of adrenaline at the end is really helpful, the quality of your work should not be sacrificed for that.

    v. Build in margin, and plan prayerfully.

    vi. Change something if it does not work.

    vii. Ask yourself and others what went well and what should change the next time this season comes back around. Do this both in the middle of the season and at the end.

Wise season planning requires that we consider who we are and how we work, as well as naming (as best we can) what the goals of the season are and how it might feel to be present within it. Season planning will always be an act of faith, but it can be done oriented toward taking good care of what we are responsible for stewarding.

### *Questions for Reflection*

1. Does your organization have a philosophy of nestedness? Why or why not? What is the effect of that decision on you in your role?
2. Which of the capabilities in organizational ecosystem nesting—influence, response to change, and adapting—do you excel at? Which is more difficult for you to practice?
3. Do you think and plan "seasonally"? Why or why not? What could more season planning look like for you?
4. How have you seen the practice of Sabbath produce health in you?

13

# Succession Planning

Reverend Ford, in the 1960 Disney classic *Pollyanna*, preaches a sermon that begins with a jarring pronouncement: "Death comes unexpectedly! And the God, Jehovah, will execute his vengeance on ye who despise his undying love and trample his benefits underfoot. The unconverted soul, the foolish children of man do miserably delude themselves in the false confidence of their own strength and wisdom. They trust to nothing but a shadow. But bear testament. Death comes unexpectedly!"[1] The preacher delivers a message of deep conviction as Pollyanna, the cheerful orphan squirming next to her severe aunt, gazes up at him, mouth agog, deeply disturbed. By the end of the movie, the town finds itself having been transformed by this young girl's own conviction that gladness, rather than fear, is the modus operandi of a well-lived life. Fortunately for us, we need not choose between Reverend Ford and Pollyanna. Death may come unexpectedly, *and* we can live with gladness in the meantime. Living with genuine gladness for Christians means we account well for our own ends.

Far too often the heads of organizations—presidents, CEOs, executive directors—assume they are keystone actors in organizational ecosystems. They go to work every day believing that if (and acting as though) something were to happen to them, inevitably everything would crumble because of how operations are structured. Sometimes they believe that even when there are structures and other leaders around them that would allow the organization to carry on excellently without them. Sometimes lower-level administrators assume the same thing. The last chapter described nesting as an antidote to crisis in the organization; this chapter will look at succession planning as an antidote to crisis with leaders.

This chapter is meant to spur us toward a right view of ourselves. One day we will die, and we will not hold our positions forever (even if sometimes we cannot yet imagine stepping down, let alone retirement). How do we work well now in light of a future that will come, timing yet unknown? "Succession planning" is the term used to describe a process of identifying the potential stakeholders in an organization who could fill important roles should an urgent need arise. Those individuals are often developed to meet various competencies or brought into decision-making processes so they gain experience and exposure to the internal workings of the organization. Succession planning allows us to gain another perspective on ensuring the right people are in the right positions, sometimes even leading to promotions or job changes that can benefit everyone. The ultimate goals of succession planning are continuity and growth for the organization.

Unfortunately, sometimes serious illness or untimely death befalls people in our organizational ecosystems. Sometimes leaders act in such a way that immediate removal from positions is required. Sometimes individuals never really consider they will retire from working—perhaps the organization or its mission means that much to them. Placing ourselves appropriately in our organizations is part of our own formation, and doing so accurately contributes to a healthy experience of succession planning for all.

Appropriate self-evaluation in the context of our ecosystem requires humility and truth. Humility is necessary because we are so easily tempted to think the ecosystem's workings revolve around us. The apostle Paul invites us to imitate Jesus's humility in Philippians 2 as an example of how our lives should look if we are in communion with the triune God. True humility is characterized by love (Philippians 2:2) with the same goal of honoring Christ. Paul describes this posture: "Instead of being motivated by selfish ambition or vanity, each of you should, in humility, be moved to treat one another as more important than yourself. Each of you should be concerned not only about your own interests, but about the interests of others as well" (Philippians 2:3–4). Paul illustrates with Jesus, who gave up the glory of heaven for the dust and disgust of Earth, all so the mission of God could be accomplished. His humiliation was in service to others.

Administration in the pursuit of imitating the humility of Christ is a high calling. It requires communion with God and sharing in his life because of the incredible difficulty of putting aside our own comfort for the sake of loving others well. It means regularly and thoroughly interrogating our own motivations to sniff out the selfish ambition and vanity that all too easily sneak in. It means asking ourselves after interactions with others if we have genuinely seen and treated them as though they are more important than ourselves and if their interests have been included and valued. It means not only beholding the glory of the risen Christ as we go throughout the day, but remembering the abasement of the servant Jesus as well.

The other side of this humility-truth coin warrants that we see ourselves honestly in the context of the ecosystem of our organization. If we don't acknowledge our actual contributions to the mission and work in which we are engaged, we may be tempted to live only in the space of seeing others, burying our own contributions. A holistic view, however, invites both a consideration of the needs of others and an acknowledgment of how my contributions affect others within the system. It means knowing the value of what I bring to the table with appropriate confidence. It means seeing how my posture affects service to others and what my particular expertise means to the organization as a whole. Diminishing those contributions ends up harming the organization in the long run because value is camouflaged and less likely to be maintained after my tenure. Burying or downplaying contributions is a form of deceit, but honest evaluation serves the ecosystem well.

Poet Wendell Berry exhorts us to humility and truth, drawing imagery from the forest:

Invest in the millennium. Plant sequoias.
Say that your main crop is the forest
that you did not plant,
that you will not live to harvest.
Say that the leaves are harvested
when they have rotted into the mold.
Call that profit. Prophesy such returns.
Put your faith in the two inches of humus
that will build under the trees
every thousand years.[2]

Investing in the millennium and planting sequoias is an invitation to work that necessitates we will never stand in the prideful posture of fully seeing the fruit of what we have done. It's an act of faith (the title of Berry's poem is "The Mad Farmer Liberation Front," reminding us that this kind of work is a little crazy, after all). Those two inches of soil that result after a thousand years is truthful—valuable in what it provides to the ecosystem but not overextending or overpromising the contribution. It's humility and truth: forests do not grow by the sweat of our brow. We cultivate, taking good care of the space, but our will alone does not produce trees.

### *Feedback Loops*

Administration enacted with humility and expressed truthfully is a beautiful thing. One of the best means of truthful evaluation is through feedback loops. We use these regularly in our common experience, but setting out the process can be especially helpful in succession planning. Feedback loops require input into a system—data or information about it. Then, information is caught and expressed in some way so we can evaluate it. Next, changes can be made based on the captured data, and the process repeats. Positive change may occur when a particular change is amplified in a particular direction or a negative change is engaged to counteract something. The goal in either direction is stability and flourishing. Feedback loops help us understand the impact of various changes on the organization by using solid data to help foster resilience.

There are a number of different kinds of feedback loops present for individuals within organizations. There are spaces where formal data is provided, such as annual reviews by supervisors and 360-degree evaluations that others provide for us. Informal data can be gathered from hallway conversations, emails after a presentation, and more. When we are talking about this idea of succession planning, the goal is to gather helpful feedback from trustworthy sources, which contributes to as clear a picture as possible of the value provided. Finding trustworthy sources is part of putting together the evaluation schema.

Once accurate data is provided about our role in the organization, we have sometimes explicitly, but more often implicitly, provided motivation to incorporate that feedback into meaningful change. Then, more feedback can be gathered about effectiveness. Feedback loops relating to people within systems should be handled with care. One-to-one correlations between input and output are almost impossible, so we should expect nuance and the opportunity to parse out the context even as we engage in evaluation. For example, when a process for event planning works well in one situation, if I transfer that same process to different committee members, or even just repeat the same process with the same people the next year, there's no guarantee the result will be replicated.

Feedback loops are foundational to succession planning as we attempt to develop individuals to fill key roles. What a person brings to an organization cannot be captured in a resumé or application, so we need a more comprehensive process. Feedback loops allow us insight into what could be buried, ignored, or not yet revealed as successors engage with a variety of individuals in the organization, whether supervisors, mentors, supervisees, etc. A feedback loop that functions in the same vein as Philippians 2, out of love, honoring Christ and others, serves everyone well.

### *Life Cycles of Organizational Ecosystems*

Another key aspect of successful succession planning is understanding the life stage of the organization. Awareness of an individual's strengths and fit is important. Being cognizant of the phases of life the organization is both in now and will be in the future is also necessary in order to match the right person to the right time. For example, someone who excels during a start-up phase will most likely be frustrated in a more mature phase of the organization.

There are two foundational phases for organizational ecosystems—emerging systems and mature systems. Emerging systems need to quickly move into focusing on growth, and mature systems will eventually lead to a time of decline (or else renewal, in order to start the cycle all over again). Emerging systems can feel very loose and flexible—ideas flow, resources are chased, and little coordination is present. Most likely there is a central figure who wields power. Systems focused on growth survive on informal communication and structure, and the group can move together because of size and mission buy-in. Innovation and commitment are still very present. When an organization moves into maturity, those structures become cemented and stable. Everyone seems to talk about efficiency. Finally, an organizational ecosystem may wobble on the precipice of decline or renewal—will structures adapt, or will they rigidly stifle everyone? Will things centralize, expand, contract, change, or become latent?[3]

Being aware of the life stage of the organization allows for clarity in succession planning. One of the most noteworthy successions in Scripture is that of Moses to Joshua as the Israelites entered into the promised land. Moses, the initial leader for this emerging ecosystem, had formational experiences as a younger person that sustained him in the difficult times. He observed the unjust and abusive treatment of the Egyptians toward his own people (Exodus 5), and, when he was called to address it, even in his fear, he chose to engage because of Yahweh's presence and directives (Exodus 6:1–7:6). Moses took heed of his father-in-law's advice to build an efficient leadership structure (Exodus 18) as the organization developed into more maturity.

Joshua had the opportunity to watch Moses's leadership and learn from him. He also scouted the land (Numbers 13) and led the military (Joshua 5), so he stepped into this role with helpful prior experience and an understanding of the place Yahweh led them. Joshua no doubt heard all of Moses's parting words firsthand as Moses neared the end of his leadership tenure (which is basically the book of Deuteronomy). Moses blessed and exhorted Joshua: "Be strong and courageous, for you will accompany these people to the land that the LORD promised to give their ancestors, and you will enable them to inherit it. The LORD is indeed going before you—he will be with you; he will not fail you or abandon you. Do not be afraid or discouraged!" (Deuteronomy 31:7–8). While Moses initially struggled with some delegation and administrative tasks, Joshua seemed to be very clear about how to set up clear structures and delineation of space and tasks. That was what was needed in this era of growth and maturity in the life stage of this organizational ecosystem.

Moses was no doubt surprised when the Lord prohibited him from entering the promised land. I wonder if he wrestled with disappointment over that. God very graciously gave him the opportunity to see the entire place toward which he had walked for the past forty years, even though he could not set foot in it (Deuteronomy 34:1–4). Joshua's official entrance into the promised land (after his scouting trip) was a bold welcome from the Lord that affirmed his leadership, giftings, and trust of God. He walked across the Jordan River on dry land and dramatically felled Jericho (Joshua 2–3 and 6). Joshua was "full of the spirit of wisdom, for Moses had placed his hands on him; and the Israelites listened to him and did just what the LORD had commanded Moses" (Deuteronomy 34:9).

As Reverend Ford preached, death comes unexpectedly. Sometimes changes in leadership do as well. However, whatever the nature of the change, our challenge is similar to what Pollyanna preached as well. Will we be glad, regardless of the circumstance? Will we look for the good, finding joy in whatever comes? Preparing for these kinds of changes by listening well and discerning with humility and truth leads us to an experience of gladness.

### *Tool Kit: Developing Handbooks*

Handbooks are the documents that no one reads until we need them, but we're always happy to have them when we lack guidelines and direction. We need them updated, but the time needed to update them is hard to find. We need information at our fingertips but sometimes forget to record the changes when decisions occur. It sounds like a bad riddle: What is forgotten most of the time, necessary all the time, and a pain to update? Handbooks!

A good handbook is a comprehensive guide for how to exist in the organization and gives direction for acting in various situations and accessing resources. It is about conduct, action, and help. A handbook should be simple to use and understand, housed where it's easy to access, and organized in a logical way.

There are two keys to successful handbook development: collaboration and regular updating. Whether writing a handbook for the first time or reengaging an existing one, both cooperation and systematic review are foundational. There are lots of ways to develop collaboration as part of the process of handbook development, and how that is done will depend on the structure of the organization as well as how normal communications occur. Regular updating requires prioritization (usually scheduling in time to do so at necessary intervals—annually, biannually, etc.) and a process for doing so. For large and complex organizations, a designated project manager or project managing software can be necessary. For smaller and more centralized organizations, those tools may be helpful but not required.

An emerging organization may put off developing handbooks until its growth demands a shared understanding of policies and processes. A mature organization will enjoy the permanence of a handbook but will also have mechanisms to facilitate change in policies. Handbooks serve us, not the other way around.

My institution used to have multiple handbooks for students depending on which campus they attended. In a fit of frustration rooted in the inefficiency of our system, we decided to merge them into one handbook for all students. This required point people from each campus and each department that had a large stake in the handbook. We met to agree on the structure and contents, and set a timeline. We identified who would "own" the document's development. Then, each department merged information that had been disparately communicated and sent it to the document owner. After editing and fiddling, and leaning on external reviewers, we finalized the new handbook. Now, each June we update, sometimes tweaking the structure, but we have nothing but gratitude for how simple the work is now after that initial behemoth was felled. I just send an email asking for edits by a certain date after an initial review to get the easy items updated. I also have an electronic folder where I collect any new policies or information that needs to be included in the next year's version so it's ready to go when June comes around.

Planning for handbook development prior to a desperate need is valuable. Sometimes handbooks protect us from legal trouble; sometimes they protect us from our own poor decisions; and they almost always save us time and energy when we use them well. Handbooks are a gracious gift during times of succession—administrators exiting can ensure the structures and policies they are leaving will serve the organization well, and administrators coming in have a document formally explaining the ecosystem into which they are entering. If death does come unexpectedly, institutional memory is not lost.

### *Questions for Reflection*

1. Do you think about concluding your time at your organization in a healthy manner? If not, what could help with that?

2. How are your tendencies toward seeing yourself with humility and truthfulness? Which is more difficult for you?
3. Describe your involvement in feedback loops for both yourself and others. What are your strengths in engaging them? What could you work on?
4. In which part of the life cycle is your organization currently? How does that influence your formation? Is there anything required of you because of the stage your organization is at that you will need to pay more attention to or develop?

14

# Investing Beyond Our Years

When we leave organizations, whether through death, retirement, or other reasons, our goal should be to provide blessing for those who remain. Even when we are frustrated or hurt, the love and humility we are invited into as followers of Jesus necessitate that we leave well. "Inheritance" is the gift we receive when someone dies, and, for the purposes of this chapter, let's also consider inheritance the gift we leave behind when we depart an organization. Scripture will help us explore this topic. We'll look at several key passages to shape our understanding of inheritance and then see how we are invited to respond.

In the book of Joshua, the twelve tribes receive their inheritance in the promised land. Each tribe gets their own section of land, specifically set apart for them. The land allotment was protected by divine command and meant to be preserved for generations. It was the fulfillment of God's promise, a gift of grace, designated as such through the years, so that as each generation passed away, new people got their opportunity to make something of the land.

There was one exception, though—the tribe of Levi were not the beneficiaries of any land. The Levites were set apart for service to the Lord. God did not give them the space to build, to create, to make something *of themselves, for themselves*. However, what he gave them was much better. God promised that *he* would be their inheritance. He gave them himself. They were to serve in the temple, nearer to God than anyone else. He provided for them through the community, as the people gave their tithes and offerings to Yahweh out of their inheritance passed down through the generations.

Investing beyond our years administratively means that we do so with a sense of freedom because the success of our inheritance, the gifts we leave behind, depends entirely on God's presence in the organization. The greatest gift we can leave our organization is encouragement to trust the Lord, to listen well and follow obediently where he leads. When we model that, when we exhort others toward abiding with Christ, a sense of freedom and opportunity is connected to God's abundance, not our current situation.

There are so many references to inheritance throughout the Old Testament—the land is incredibly valuable, with laws on how to protect it from improper farming to consequences of moving boundary markers, as well as what to do if no sons are born, which is what we read about at the end of Ruth.

As Boaz is negotiating his marriage with Ruth, as well as the land and elderly woman (Naomi) who come with it, he makes a pronouncement that gets a significant mention at the end of the book. Boaz says that he has bought from Naomi all that belonged to Elimelech and his sons (Mahlon and Kilion), and also Ruth, for whom he is the kinsman redeemer. According to Ruth 4:9–10, "Then Boaz said to the leaders and all the people, 'You are witnesses today that I have acquired from Naomi all that belonged to Elimelech, Kilion, and Mahlon. I have also acquired Ruth the Moabite, the wife of Mahlon, as my wife to raise up a descendant who will inherit his property so the name of the deceased might not disappear from among his relatives and from his village. You are witnesses today'" . . . and the people affirm what Boaz has announced. Boaz has such a commitment to the value of inheritance that he emphasizes that the land he is buying will remain in Mahlon's name. He is requesting that Mahlon's inheritance be honored. A purpose of Ruth and Boaz's marriage is an heir who will ensure the inheritance remains in the family. It's an act of grace, rescuing what by rights would have disappeared.

Investing beyond our years means sometimes making costly choices that will benefit others rather than ourselves. It's sacrificial, and it means looking far ahead to the future, imagining what might happen from our Spirit-led acts of faith. Administration in *memento mori* means our name and our reputation may very well fade, but if we have invested wisely, what really matters will last.

The idea of inheritance is especially seen in Psalm 16, a reflection on what David has received from God and a pleading of what he is cognizant of still needing from Yahweh.

> [1]Keep me safe, my God,
> for in you I take refuge.
> [2]I say to the LORD, "You are my Lord;
> apart from you I have no good thing."
> [3]I say of the holy people who are in the land,
> "They are the noble ones in whom is all my delight."
> [4]Those who run after other gods will suffer more
> and more.
> I will not pour out libations of blood to such gods
> or take up their names on my lips.
> [5]LORD, you alone are my portion and my cup;
> you make my lot secure.
> [6]The boundary lines have fallen for me in pleasant places;
> surely I have a delightful inheritance.
> [7]I will praise the LORD, who counsels me;
> even at night my heart instructs me.
> [8]I keep my eyes always on the LORD.
> With him at my right hand, I will not be shaken.
> [9]Therefore my heart is glad and my tongue rejoices;
> my body also will rest secure,
> [10]because you will not abandon me to the realm of
> the dead,
> nor will you let your faithful one see decay.
> [11]You make known to me the path of life;
> you will fill me with joy in your presence,
> with eternal pleasures at your right hand. (NIV)

David begins with this request: keep me safe, protect me, guard me. He needs help—there is danger and things are precarious. He next lays out his defense for why Yahweh should help him:

- Point 1: David knows that he has nothing without the Lord—Yahweh is his only source of well-being (v. 2).
- Point 2: He's invested in God's people and is in communion with them (v. 3). It's about loyalty and care.
- Point 3: David knows that pursuing anyone other than the Lord will bring suffering, so he's resolved to not do so (v. 4). There's a correct way to go through life, and he's committed to Yahweh's way.

Why should Yahweh help him? He's dependent on the Lord, has invested in God's people, and he has the right perspective.

Then the psalmist shifts to a more personal tone of communication. In verse 5 David asserts this to Yahweh himself:

> Lord, you alone are my portion and my cup;
> you make my lot secure.

This is about stability and prosperity, using inheritance language. In the crazy world in which we live, in a situation where it feels like everything can be taken away in a moment, God is his security. This is not simply a doctrinal statement for the psalmist, though; it's close to home. He knows his need for the One who will sustain his very life.

David adds another description of what God has done for him:

> The boundary lines have fallen for me in pleasant places;
> surely I have a delightful inheritance. (v. 6)

God's provision for David is like a beautiful piece of land. In a world where corruption is present, where land is life and hope, that assurance of a place for the psalmist to dwell safely is incredibly meaningful. David knows what he has received from the Lord is a gift—

it's not something he's earned or forged out of the earth, making of himself or for himself, but he is the grateful recipient of this gift, this inheritance.

Then the psalmist shifts back to talking about the Lord—he resolves to praise the Lord, who counsels him, to keep his eyes on Yahweh.

The psalm ends with another speech directed to Yahweh. David can rejoice and be glad because God will not abandon him. The psalmist has been faithful, and the Lord will keep him vibrant and flourishing. He knows God will lead him in the best way, the way of life, which is joy with God because of nearness to God. These sentiments are memorialized in the idea of an inheritance—a gift in perpetuity. It's as if God is his inheritance.

Psalm 16 is a wonderful integration of the ideas of investing beyond our years as seen in Joshua and Ruth, coupled with worship and praise of the One who is our provider and sustainer. Will we, like the psalmist, acknowledge the gracious gift of what we have been given so that others might delight in Yahweh's presence and provision as well? Administration in *memento mori* means we offer recognition of God as our inheritance.

In Luke 1 we are introduced to a priest for whom God has officially been his inheritance for generations. Zechariah and Elizabeth are childless when we meet them, living righteously before the Lord. The one time in his life when Zechariah is picked to perform his priestly duties before Yahweh, an angel interrupts with the news that he and Elizabeth will have a delightful son who will bring much joy to everyone. Zechariah has some questions about the feasibility of this, and, as a means of transformation, is ushered into a season of divinely mandated silence. When the baby is born, in both an act of obedience to the Lord and a demonstration of Zechariah's trust in the Lord as his inheritance, the baby is not named after anyone in the family but is a signpost to how Zechariah and Elizabeth have learned to see God: the name John means "the Lord is merciful." Zechariah's song of praise demonstrates his understanding that the gift of John is part of God's plan (according to Luke 1:79) "to give light to those who sit in darkness and in the shadow of death, to guide our feet into the way of peace." This inheritance is now expanded. It is for all who are living in darkness, offering hope to everyone.

Investing beyond our years means the mission into which we have poured ourselves may change, adapting in some foundational ways. Our goal must be to give space for that to happen rather than restricting what the organization ought to be doing. Mission is not abandoned in these situations, but rather we seek the Lord to understand as best we can what he may do in the future.

In Galatians we have an inheritance twist. The inheritance is expanded to all people, but the caveat is, you still have to join the family. In Galatians 4:4–7 we find that those who have placed their faith in Christ have been adopted into God's family, with all the rights and privileges thereunto. Jesus is the executor of the inheritance of God. Our inheritance comes through him—he is the embodiment of blessings that come from God. He is the true heir of the inheritance, *and* we can know him as friend and brother. "But when the appropriate time had come, God sent out his Son, born of a woman, born under the law, to redeem those who were under the law, so that we may be adopted as sons with full rights. And because you are sons, God sent the Spirit of his Son into our hearts, who calls 'Abba! Father!' So you are no longer a slave but a son, and if you are a son, then you are also an heir through God" (Galatians 4:4–7). For those who are part of the family, the inheritance is secure.

Investing beyond our years can be joy. The same assurance of our adoption into God's family is not replicated as organizational success in perpetuity. Rather, administration in *memento mori* includes that wide-open sense of trusting the Lord with everything, believing that Jesus's power and wisdom will lead us. We can trust God to accomplish his intended work in our world. Our privilege and delight is partnering with him. That is our inheritance, the gift we leave behind.

While spiritual inheritance is far better than whatever we leave behind in our work or ministry, unless we understand these biblical foundations for what leaving things behind is meant to do for us, we may miss the richness of the experience that God intends. When someone leaves an organization, we may have a mix of emotions: grief, relief, fear, joy, and more. Reflection on the intersection of spiritual inheritance and organizational departure is valuable.

When we are disappointed that a person leaves, even when we can acknowledge their contributions to the organizational ecosystem, that never replaces *them*. Jesus is the gift of the inheritance, and we will always have him. He never leaves us. We do not have to *miss* anything about him because he died.

When we are disappointed by the work and suffering from leaving, Jesus comes to us freely, as a gift of the deepest grace imaginable. It is inevitable that someone dying, retiring, or leaving an organization will result in more work and more stress for those who remain. The contrast with Jesus is remarkable. Jesus's love, kindness, and companionship come to us with a simple ask. There's no going through old files trying to find an important piece of information. There's no loss of knowledge or skill or the heavy burden of picking up responsibilities that have been left. There's just benevolent goodness and mercy and love—right there for us.

Remember the gifts of Jesus that are ours now. We have the gift of his Spirit, the privilege of being part of his church, and the joy of mission and purpose. Let's live well with those gifts. We ought to have the posture of gratitude. As Paul wrote to the Galatians: we can truly say, "Abba! Father!" With joy, we can anticipate the full reception of our inheritance that will one day be ours in eternity.

Remember the hope in Revelation 21:5–8: "And the one seated on the throne said: 'Look! I am making all things new!' Then he said to me, 'Write it down, because these words are reliable and true.' He also said to me, 'It is done! I am the Alpha and the Omega, the beginning and the end. To the one who is thirsty I will give water free of charge from the spring of the water of life. The one who conquers will inherit these things, and I will be his God and he will be my son.'" The hope of inheritance is that, out of our identity as stakeholders in the ecosystem of the kingdom of God, we will be able to contribute to God's purposes on Earth beyond our tenure at any specific organization. We have the privilege of building contributions that can go beyond our limited time. Our contributions can create space for growth, for innovation and creativity, for making something of whatever "land" our organizations have.

### *Tool Kit: Developing Young People*

A wonderful way of leaving an inheritance is to focus on developing young people. Year after year I find myself waffling between growing delight in young people and bafflement at them and how they engage with work and the world. My face often reflects (hopefully kindly) bewilderment as I try to understand a different way of thinking or working.

It's important to name how we understand the goal of "developing" young people. Developing is not making a carbon copy of oneself. Developing is not giving someone a position and resources and then just letting them go at it. Rather, developing someone is the opportunity to know them well so we can invite them into more. Thus, they flourish, as does the organizational ecosystem.

What follows are some of the key anchors for developing young people and their administrative intelligence.

1. Begin with relationship. Understanding who they are and how they see the world is foundational. Doing this takes a lot of time and a lot of questions. Knowing their story and motivations will anchor the relationship.
2. Give them as much freedom as possible. Great ideas need to percolate, so if we come in with boundaries too early, creativity is stifled.
3. Ask *all* the questions. When curiosity motivates questions, they are often welcomed with great exuberance. Wondering about various reasons for choices, trying to ascertain how a certain direction will land with others, inquiring how the young person has accounted for resource acquisition, etc., all help with the goal of development.
4. Share the vision. Explaining the hope and the end goal for whatever

the context requires is crucial. Sometimes there might be persuasion involved, as the young person might need more than a simple statement on what the vision is, but they may be open to considering any compelling reasons for why the vision matters.

5. Invite them into the work. Young people have an uphill challenge to develop themselves outside of having the identity of a consumer. Living into a vision requires action, and passivity is a large hill to climb toward that.
6. Maintain a sense of humor. Keeping laughter at the forefront is important because each of you will have moments of getting frustrated with the other. Merriment in those moments will help smooth things over and give perspective when needed.

One of the best hires I ever made involved an interesting path of development. This young person took my "Administration for Ministry" class during his time in seminary. He was a good student and helpfully engaged in the topics, asking thoughtful questions. I knew from his final project that he was contemplating ministry in an educational environment. A year later, just after he graduated, I was looking for a coordinator for the Student Life department. I had some specific qualifications in mind, and this seemed like a great opportunity to hire someone who had an interest in the field but little experience. The position did not pay a lot, but I was willing to provide development with the hope of opening up opportunities for that person.

After posting the position, I sent my former student an email encouraging him to apply. We received some wonderful candidates with a lot of potential. After we walked through our hiring process, he was our person. It was unique to bring someone in who had already heard and reflected upon my personal convictions about administrative work, already read several of the books that I consider valuable, and now was in a position to evaluate firsthand if I walked the walk or just talked the talk.

The first year of our weekly meetings included a lot of time explaining why I thought Student Life should function the way we were building it and how those abstract administrative principles applied to our context. We envisioned together his contribution to theological education generally and what his role specifically could look like. We laughed, asked a million clarifying questions, and listened well to each other. His contributions are going beyond Student Life to other areas of the school, and we're talking now about next steps in his position.

The administrative assistant in our department and I will often tell each other, "If I'm hit by a bus . . ." and then give a piece of random information that may be needed in such a scenario. (She has also now started to say, "If I get to go be with Jesus" as a more Christian approach.) If I do unexpectedly get to go and be with the Lord, I want to be confident that I've done everything I can to help those left behind to carry on in what we've all chosen to invest. That's administration in *memento mori*.

### *Questions for Reflection*

1. How would you name the gifts you are leaving behind for your organization if you were suddenly taken away?
2. If you could start over, what gifts to leave behind would you focus your attention on now?
3. What does developing young people look like for you at this stage? What are your joys and challenges in working with them?
4. How have you seen young people respond to your development of them?

Conclusion

# Taken Care Of

The garden of Eden was a thriving, vibrant ecosystem . . . for however long it took for Adam and Eve to succumb to the suggestions of the serpent. And then, the whole ecosystem was corrupted. Eden was irreparably ruined because the stewards were self-serving; they walked away from communion with their Creator, and the seed of sin and evil grew from there. What does that mean for us now?

At this point in cosmic history, we aim for faithfulness to the identity and tasks that we have been given, meanwhile waiting with hope for all to be remade so that corruption is replaced by what can never be destroyed. When we are convinced of our belovedness, that the God of the universe rejoices over us with singing (Zephaniah 3:17), that nothing changes his delight in us, then we are living as one formed for the good of the world—and that's what flows from all our work.

In part 1 we looked at work in an ecosystem—good decisions, good change, and coordinating conflict—the essential work of administrators who carefully steward people, resources, and projects through a process. In part 2 we looked at cultivation—artifacts, hospitality, and proper presence—as the tools of curation by the administrator. Part 3 brought us into the realm of fruitfulness, which is the goal of the ecosystem. We examined challenges toward fruitfulness and being formed by prayer. In part 4 we explored an approach to solving problems by developing our imaginative capacities and taking good care of our ecosystems through design thinking. Our final section was an invitation to think about administration in light of our eventual death, preparing well for our exit from the organization at some unknown point.

What kind of people are able to take good care of the organizational ecosystems of which they are a part? The ones who themselves have experienced good care from God—they are secure in their belovedness and live out of that identity and rootedness. They are listening to the Spirit of God, following the directions of God, for the sake of the glory of God. When we are convinced to the very core of our being that God takes good care of us, we can overflow with the kind of work that demonstrates our rootedness in the steadfast love God has shown to us.

A well-cared-for ecosystem has each part functioning in the manner in which it is intended, bearing fruit in its season, connected to the whole. We, the administrators and gardeners, seek to do our part in cultivating this space, but at the end of the day we brush the dirt off our clothes, wash our hands, and go home, only to find that when we return the next morning and inspect the garden, new blooms have arrived, or we spy a seed that has germinated and is peeking up through the soil. All of this happened while we were away. This is the work of the Spirit of God.

Paul's testimony in 1 Corinthians 3:6–7 is that he performed his role, but God is the one who caused the seeds to grow. Our job is faithful stewarding the people, resources, and projects for which we have responsibility. God's job is the rest. Faithfully stewarding ourselves means that we pay attention to our own formation and to the ways we are being shaped by the organization, pushing back against what is not of the Lord, welcoming what is, waiting, and working with wise boundaries. We have an opportunity for contextualized formation—not abstract but grounded in the work we do day in and day out. This is God's blessing for us—that he would bless the world through our work.

Ecosystems emerge from the ground up (quite literally) as organisms develop and adapt so that the system eventually teems with life. This is where we detect the impressive work of the Holy Spirit. The

Spirit is present in the beginning, moving and developing, and the Spirit is present as flourishing growth occurs. The Spirit works before and within and at the end. Our peace and our hope is that while the master plan may be hidden from us, God is working always and everywhere to accomplish what he intends. This is the "life abundant" Jesus promised, and it is ours in him. We take good care because God has taken good care of us.

### *Questions for Reflection*

1. How are you grappling with living in a reality that is less than the Edenic ideal?
2. What kind of a plan for your contextualized formation has emerged?
3. What would it look like for you to lean more into the Spirit of God in his role in the ecosystem?
4. What are some ways you've seen God take good care of you recently?

# Acknowledgments

I have been taken good care of by so many people. Incredible teachers have formed me, and I am thankful for your investment. I'm grateful to have worked in the organizations that have shaped me and offered space to practice my administrative imagination. The Lord's providence and kindness are extraordinarily evident to me.

While this is a completely obnoxious choice since I could go on and on, I'm going to name just a few people in gratitude for their influence on the particular topics in this book. Thank you to Felix and Esther Theonugraha, Jim Moore, Linda Cannell, Donald and Mary Guthrie, Deb Colwill, Stacy Lung, Jeannette Hsieh, Brad Howell, Jon Ro, and Herb Ahne.

Writing has been a delight—what fun to have a supergroup of cheerleaders assembled: Amber Nakamura, Christine Lee, Rebecca Eunha Kim Moon, Wendy Murray, Pat Batten, Eun Ah Cho, Gwen McWhorter, Natalie Crowson, Jeff and Teal Wojciki, and Dawn Bryden. I'm so grateful for the excellent help and skills Sydney Hughes offered. Thank you to my family (Donna, Lainey, Jared, Bridger, Marisa, Ashok, Amos, Mara, Jarin, and Inna) for being supportive and proud of me in your unique ways. I'm grateful to Ronda Jones, who let me know that my dad told her he thought I needed to write a book. I wish he would have known.

# Notes

### *Chapter 1*

1. Unless otherwise indicated, biblical quotations come from the New English Translation.

2. The best teacher on how to make decisions that I've come across is Emily P. Freeman, particularly in her book *The Next Right Thing* (she also has a podcast by the same name with other reflections on aspects of decision making). So much of how I think about decision making has been shaped by her work, and I'm so grateful. What follows is a contextualization based on her wise work. Emily P. Freeman, *The Next Right Thing* (Revell, 2019).

3. Emily P. Freeman has developed a guided journal that is a wonderful tool for developing our acumen for reflection. *The Next Right Thing Guided Journal: A Decision-Making Companion* (Revell, 2021).

4. Chip Heath and Dan Heath, *Decisive: How to Make Better Choices in Life and Work* (Crown Currency, 2013). In the first "Administration for Ministry" course I taught at Gordon-Conwell Theological Seminary, we had a very helpful discussion on this, and credit goes to the students in that course for their help in thinking this through, particularly (in my memory) to Bennett and TJ.

5. Lester Edwin J. Ruiz, "I Believe in the Resurrection of the Body—Meditations and Explorations on 'The Religious,' 'The Public,' and the Asian Diaspora: A Research Framework and Agenda" (paper for the Conference on Religions and Asian Public Life, Chung Chui College, Chinese University of Hong Kong, July 6–7, 2012), 5.

6. Dallas Willard, *Renovation of the Heart* (NavPress, 2002), 105.

7. Gordon T. Smith, *Listening to God in Times of Choice* (InterVarsity Press, 1997), 25.

8. Marva J. Dawn, *Joy in Divine Wisdom* (Jossey-Bass, 2006), 18.

9. Dawn, *Joy in Divine Wisdom*, 20.

10. It can be quite difficult when someone asks you to perform a delegated task but you do not think that is appropriate. In these situations an honest conversation is important, explaining your perspective and hearing theirs. Sometimes it can be helpful to negotiate (if I take delegated task X, could I be exempt from normal task Y?), or to ask for an incentive or benefit. Sometimes these approaches work, sometimes they do not; sometimes bringing in a supervisor or mediator is necessary. It also might be the case that wisdom leads to just taking it on and hoping for the best.

11. In my education classes at Trinity Evangelical Divinity School, Dr. Donald Guthrie often referred to this metaphor for how to engage with students. I've found it to be exceedingly helpful and have benefited from his wise teaching and reflection.

12. There are ethical concerns related to the use of some nondisclosure agreements (NDAs) because they can silence victims in abuse situations, allowing the offending party to continue problematic behaviors. Covering up mistreatment or abuse through NDAs is abhorrent. Using an NDA when it's clear that the departing employee is likely to use resources to benefit a competitor is understandable. An NDA should be transparent, specific about information and time, and not overly broad.

### *Chapter 2*

1. There's a caveat to be noted here, in that interpersonal conflict should be dealt with in a less public manner to begin with, following Jesus's outline in Matthew 19.

2. There is some argument among scholars that he didn't actually create this model, but others put it together from his work after his death in 1947.

3. Kurt Lewin, "Group Decision and Social Change," in *The Complete Social Scientist: A Kurt Lewin Reader*, ed. Martin Gold (American Psychological Association, 1999), 265–84.

4. John Kotter, "The Eight Steps for Leading Change," Kotter, accessed May 7, 2025, https://tinyurl.com/kczcfvrh.

5. Ronald Heifetz and Marty Linsky, "A Survival Guide for Leaders," *Harvard Business Review*, June 2002, https://tinyurl.com/3fap4ay2.

### *Chapter 3*

1. Ann Garrido's excellent book, *Redeeming Power* (Ave Maria Press, 2024), walks through various kinds of power expressed in institutions. It is a profound reflection, and I highly recommend it as a guide to further explore power in an ecosystem.

2. Bob Burns, Tasha Chapman, and Donald C. Guthrie, *Politics of Ministry* (InterVarsity Press, 2019), 18.

3. Credit to Burns, Chapman, and Guthrie for not only this term but also for a turn in my thinking about politics in Christian contexts.

4. Burns, Chapman, and Guthrie, *Politics of Ministry*, 21.

5. Burns, Chapman, and Guthrie, *Politics of Ministry*, 27, describe negotiation using four activities (people bring their own interests to the process, promote their interests between each other, use the power available to promote their interests, and affect ongoing interests and power by their actions during and after the negotiation). I have expanded these activities in my explanation but certainly give credit to these authors for the foundation.

6. Joshua Jipp, *Saved by Faith and Hospitality* (Eerdmans, 2017), 2.

7. Christine D. Pohl, *Living into Community: Cultivating Practices That Sustain Us* (Eerdmans, 2012), 159.

8. Selections from Rebecca R. Hernandez, "Beyond 'Hospitality': Moving Out of the Host-Guest Metaphor into an Intercultural 'World House,'" in *Thriving in Leadership: Strategies for Making a Difference in Christian Higher Education*, ed. Karen Longman (Abilene Christian University Press, 2012), 223–40.

9. Whenever I read Dr. Hernandez's article I have the Newsboys' song "Big House" running through my head.

### Chapter 4

1. Andy Crouch, *Culture Making* (InterVarsity Press, 2008), 24.

2. Crouch, *Culture Making*, 29. We've been talking about tangible and intangible "stuff." Crouch's artifacts discussion applies to both categories well.

3. Crouch, *Culture Making*, 29–30.

4. Crouch, *Culture Making*, 75.

5. Crouch, *Culture Making*, 77.

6. Crouch, *Culture Making*, 90.

### Chapter 5

1. Unreasonable Hospitality, accessed November 8, 2024, https://tinyurl.com/4jyk3je5.

2. Will Guidara, *Unreasonable Hospitality: The Remarkable Power of Giving People More Than They Expect* (Optimism Press, 2022).

3. Hernandez, "Beyond 'Hospitality,'" 229.

4. Craig Dykstra, "The Pastoral Imagination," *Initiatives in Religion* 9, no. 1 (2001): 1.

### Chapter 6

1. D. Randy Garrison, Terry Anderson, and Walter Archer, "Critical Thinking, Cognitive Presence, and Computer Conferencing in Distance Education," May 4, 2004, https://tinyurl.com/4fmk8emr, 5.

2. Garrison, Anderson, and Archer, "Critical Thinking," 5.

3. My theology professor in seminary lectured on Torrance's Trinitarian approach, and this quote has stayed with me the last twenty years. Unfortunately, I have been unable to find the exact quote from Torrance but wish to provide credit for such a profound statement.

### Chapter 7

1. It is worth noting that "challenge" is helpful in a system, but danger, by definition, is prohibiting the flourishing of the system and ought not to

be present. It takes much wisdom and seeking the Lord to discern when challenge morphs into danger. Agreed-upon markers of when that happens ought to be discussed. For example, sometimes God invites us to stay in a challenging context for the sake of our being stretched, but knowing beforehand what toxicity looks and feels like is important.

2. John F. Kilner, *Dignity and Destiny: Humanity in the Image of God* (Eerdmans, 2015), 311.

3. L. Gregory Jones, "Forgiveness," in *Practicing Our Faith: A Way of Life for a Searching People*, ed. Dorothy C. Bass (Wiley & Sons, 1997), 133.

4. Someone may have lying or cheating behaviors that ought to be addressed, but forgiveness is not dependent on that occurring.

5. Jones, "Forgiveness," 135.

6. Jones, "Forgiveness," 138–39.

7. Jones, "Forgiveness," 140.

8. Kevin Vanhoozer, "The Voice and the Actor," in *Evangelical Futures*, ed. John G. Stackhouse (Baker Books, 2000), 84.

9. Kevin Vanhoozer and Owen Strachan, *The Pastor as Public Theologian: Reclaiming a Lost Vision* (Baker Academic, 2015), 111.

### Chapter 8

1. "Mission & Money: Leaning into Reality & Leading a Seminary out of Debt," Gordon Conwell Theological Seminary, press release, May 13, 2021, https://tinyurl.com/mu69nwdb.

2. John W. Wimberly Jr., *The Business of the Church* (Alban Institute, 2010), 7.

### Chapter 9

1. Jim Wilder and Michel Hendricks, *The Other Half of Church* (Moody, 2020).

2. Wilder and Hendricks, *The Other Half*, 20.

3. Wilder and Hendricks, *The Other Half*, 23 and 28.

4. Ken Blanchard, William Oncken Jr., and Hal Burrows, *The One Minute Manager Meets the Monkey* (William Morrow, 1999).

### *Part 4*

1. https://tinyurl.com/ycx5xbmw, accessed November 15, 2024.

2. Gregory Currie and Ian Ravenscroft, *Recreative Minds* (Clarendon, 2003), 1.

3. Currie and Ravenscroft, *Recreative Minds*, 1.

4. Luci Shaw, *Breath for the Bones: Art, Imagination, and Spirit; A Reflection on Art, Creativity, and Faith* (Nelson, 2009), 81.

5. Wendell Berry, "Sabbath," in *A Small Porch: Sabbath Poems, 2014–2015* (Counterpoint, 2017).

### *Chapter 10*

1. These suggestions originated from my dissertation research, studying administrators in theological education who have what I termed "administrative imagination." I'm grateful to have learned from such wise and erudite professionals.

2. JoAnn Franklin Klinker, "Imagination," in *Encyclopedia of Educational Leadership and Administration*, ed. Fenwick W. English (Sage, 2006), 494.

3. Klinker, "Imagination," 494.

### *Chapter 11*

1. Tom Kelley, *The Art of Innovation: Lessons in Creativity from IDEO, America's Leading Design Firm* (Doubleday, 2001).

2. Kelley, *The Art of Innovation*, 6–7.

3. IDEO, accessed May 14, 2025, https://tinyurl.com/bdepr4av.

4. For a helpful overview, see Designing Your Life, accessed May 14, 2025, https://tinyurl.com/4b4hbnbx.

### *Part 5*

1. "Millennials or Gen Z: Who's Doing the Most Job-Hopping," Career Builder, accessed May 15, 2025, https://tinyurl.com/2u2x6kwk.

2. "Median Tenure with Current Employers was 3.5 Years in Private Sector in January 2024," U.S. Bureau of Labor Statistics, April 9, 2025, https://tinyurl.com/ydsh5afh.

### *Chapter 12*

1. While it worked for a number of years, since then the church has gone back to meeting in one location. Changes in staffing and leadership dynamics contributed significantly to this shift.

2. Matthew M. Mars, Judith L. Bronstein, and Robert F. Lush, "The Value of a Metaphor: Organizations and Ecosystems," *Organizational Dynamics* 41, no. 4 (October 2012): 273.

3. Mars, Bronstein, and Lush, "The Value of a Metaphor," 273.

4. "Student Services" is the umbrella department of which Student Life, Student Success, Registration, and various other offices are usually considered a part, although there can be some variety in how schools organize themselves.

5. See Peter Wohlleben, *The Hidden Life of Trees: What They Feel, How They Communicate* (Collins, 2016), for a wonderful exploration of how an ecosystem exhibits this.

6. Nicolai J. Foss, Jens Schmidt, and David J. Teece, "Ecosystem Leadership as a Dynamic Capability," *Long Range Planning* 56 (2023): 7.

7. I owe a debt of gratitude to Kendra Adachi and her "Lazy Genius" approach, having read her book *The Lazy Genius Way: Embrace What Matters, Ditch What Doesn't, and Get Stuff Done* (WaterBrook, 2020) and listened to her podcast for years. I've adapted her approach to the context of administration and certainly owe her credit for many of the principles here.

8. I want to emphasize that practicing Sabbath does not guarantee that

burnout will be avoided, nor should we practice it with that motivation, but rather Sabbath is blessed in and of itself, as God declared in Genesis 2:3.

### *Chapter 13*

1. *Pollyanna,* David Swift, Disney, 1960. View the scene at https://tinyurl.com/yx8bf9za.

2. Wendell Berry, "Manifesto: The Mad Farmer Liberation Front," All Poetry, accessed May 16, 2025, https://tinyurl.com/4tm8tut3.

3. David S. Bright et al., *Principles of Management* (self-published, 2019), https://tinyurl.com/42adk678, section 10.2.